bordeaux and bicycles

by

Steven Herrick

Table of Contents

About the Author

Steven Herrick is the author of twenty-one books for children and young adults. In Australia, his books have won the New South Wales Premier's Literary Award in 2000 and 2005 and the Western Australia Premier's Literary Award in 2013. His books have also been shortlisted for the prestigious Children's Book Council of Australia Book of the Year Awards on seven occasions. He is published in the USA by Simon and Schuster and Boyds Mill Press. He has also been published in the UK and The Netherlands.

Steven has written travel articles and features for newspapers and magazines and regularly travels the world performing his poetry and conducting author talks in schools. He lives in the Blue Mountains in Australia with his wife, Cathie, a belly dance teacher. They have two adult sons, Jack and Joe.

This is his second travel book, following on from the successful, *baguettes and bicycles*.

www.stevenherrick.com.au

dothebikething.blogspot.com.au

Introduction

In 2012, I cycled across the width of France, from west to east, beginning in Saint Nazaire on the Atlantic Coast and finishing in Basel, Switzerland. It was eighteen days of relaxed cycling and extensive eating. Huge breakfasts, frequent visits to boulangeries, three-course lunches and four-course dinners were necessary fuel for the kilometres I cycled.

Or so I told myself.

In truth, I was enjoying the variety and quality of French food as much as the fabulous scenery and the pleasant cycle paths.

I christened my red hybrid bicycle, Craig, after the surname of a well-known weight-loss guru. Well, I could hardly ride *Jenny* across France, could I? This French adventure became the basis of my travel memoir, *baguettes and bicycles*, which was subsequently published in late-2012

Arriving back in Australia, I weighed myself, with trepidation. I had gained only one kilogram! I celebrated with a visit to the local baker who creates croissants almost as tasty as his French brothers. I told my wife all about my cycling adventures and relived each delicious meal in minute detail.

A few weeks later, she suggested the idea of buying a bicycle for herself. I was ecstatic! We chose a light-blue drop-bar Giant with twenty-one gears and an easy disposition. She was christened 'Patootie,' rhymes with *cutie*.

My wife is a bellydancer which means balance and core strength are easy for her. She rode down Narrow Neck Road with the polished grace of a professional.

Cathie and I started discussing possible cycling holidays. Her bellydance teaching would be put on hold for a few months. She was swapping swirling skirts, bare midriffs, veils and bundles of costume jewellery for lycra, fingerless gloves and flat-soled shoes.

Our first holiday was in rural Victoria, riding along an old rail trail between historic towns. The daily expedition was sixty kilometres, punctuated by cafe stops and photo opportunities. It's a pity that the region was experiencing heatwave conditions. Cathie's cycle began earlier each morning as the temperature soared to over 40 degrees celsius by 10am. Occasionally, I accompanied her, but mostly I threw my road bike into the back of the car and drove to the nearby Australian Alps, where I tackled a different mountain climb each day, before the heat became too intense. It was the perfect holiday - food and wine, flat tracks for Cathie and peaks for me.

On the long drive home, we filled in the time with thoughts of where we could cycle next holiday.

'Why don't we land in Paris and cycle home,' I suggested.

Cathie smiled. 'Via Afghanistan, or Iran and Iraq,' she answered.

'Always the opportunity for bellydancing,' I suggested. 'Or we could cycle across the Northern Stans and through China.'

'All this after riding 60 kilometres a day for five days,' she said. 'Perhaps something a little less...'

'Exotic,' I suggested.

'Long,' Cathie added.

We drove in silence, both thinking of shorter, easier alternatives.

'Italy?' I offered.

'Too many hills,' Cathie replied.

'But you love Italian food,' I pleaded.

'Then why not France,' Cathie asked, 'I love French food over everything.'

'Even over dancing?'

'Even over you!'

We both laughed.

So, it was settled.

France.

'I'd rather not do the Loire again,' I said.

Cathie thought for a few moments.

'Remember that English chef who travelled on barges across the south of France,' she asked.

'Rick somebody,' I couldn't remember his surname.

'That's him,' she clicked her fingers, 'Rick *Somebody*! If there's a canal, I imagine there's a cycle path close by.'

'From the Atlantic to the Mediterranean. Perfect!' I said. 'We'll start at the ocean and cycle easy paths all the way to the sea.'

For the next few weeks, I pored over maps, plotting the best course. Finally, I decided on beginning at Lake Arcachon on the Atlantic Coast and heading vaguely south-east along a cycle path, until we'd make a sharp left turn and sweep across twenty kilometres of backwoods French roads before joining the Canal de Garonne at its starting point near the village of Langon. From there it would be cycle paths all the way to Toulouse where we'd join the Canal du Midi for an easy pedal to the Mediterranean. A quick check of Google confirmed the route was approximately seven hundred kilometres, spiced with regular detours to vineyards, boulangeries and hill-top villages.

'We'll eat our way through Southern France,' I said, 'And gain only one kilogram each.'

Cathie shot me a glance that suggested I should not mention weight during the trip.

'You can afford to gain lots, if you want,' I helpfully suggested.

Cathie did her best Marge Simpson-like growl.

No more talk of weight gains.

Or punctures.

Or rain storms.

Or wind squalls.

It would be easy kilometres, highlighted by visits to boulangeries, cafes and cosy Chambre d'Hotes. Rick Somebody would be proud.

Chapter One

Lake Arcachon to Canal de Garonne

We arrived in Paris a few days ago, leased a car and drove to a bed and breakfast in Saint-Firmin-sur-Loire where I had a tearful reunion with Craig, my bicycle, who had been resting in a barn since the previous summer. Craig appeared happy to see me. Well he didn't get a puncture on our first reunion cycle of a few kilometres along the Loire. In fact, for a bicycle that had spent a cold winter freezing in an unheated barn, he positively purred. I promised him chain oil and warm lodgings for the next month.

We'd also stopped at a Decathlon sports store to buy Cathie a bike. She chose a 21-gear silver and black model, we christened, appropriately, *Jenny*.

Jenny and Craig.

Together they would transport us willingly over endless canal paths and allow us to eat multiple-course lunches and dinners without gaining weight. Craig appeared happy to have a travelling companion, although he did grumble a little about carrying the bulk of our clothes in his panniers, allowing Jenny and Cathie to speed ahead with only lightweight baggage. He can be a little lacking in manners, sometimes. Perhaps like his rider.

With Craig and Jenny sharing the back seat, we drove from Saint-Firmin to Lake Arcachon on the Atlantic Coast. Jenny and Craig spent their first night together in the back of a Citroen Picasso, like fondling adolescents, while Cathie and I made do with a roadside hotel.

****

The morning dawns cold and bleak, with rain sweeping in from the ocean. For the first day of this journey, Craig and I are alone.

Cathie is driving the car inland from Lake Arcachon to find suitable accommodation where we can leave the vehicle for a few weeks while we cycle to the Mediterranean. The criteria she's been given is a farmhouse with lots of space.

'It should be easy,' I say, as I wave her goodbye.

She speeds off in the Citroen and Craig immediately begins whining about Jenny getting a free ride while he does all the work. I remind him that *I'll* be doing the pedalling. He only has to travel in a vaguely straight line from here to the Canal de Garonne.

The Bassin d'Arcachon is a sweep of tidal lake and coastal holiday homes from the glitzy Cap Ferret where Zidedine Zidane has a mansion to the more down-at-heel Le Teste de Buch where Craig and I begin our journey. Nearby is the famous Dune of Pilat, at 107 metres high, the tallest sand dune in Europe and home to trudging tourists and biting winds. Cathie and I climbed the dune in 2008 and were hugely impressed by the glorious views and wheezing tourists at the point of heart failure. It really was a grand lump of sand. I could almost imagine myself as Lawrence of Arabia, savouring the expanse of water on the horizon. Was that the Atlantic? Or a mirage of Biblical proportions? After fighting our way through the tatty stalls selling tourist junk at the foot of the dune, we drove to Arcachon and were equally stunned by the cost of a coffee in summer season. We'd need the income of a World-Cup-winning footballer to live here. Farewell Zizou!

Although it's technically summer now, the weather is against Craig and me. I'm wearing a gore-tex jacket over my lycra and after only five minutes of cycling along a bumpy path, I'm cold and my gloves are already soaked. Craig has a mysterious squeak that perhaps has something to do with a lack of oil and the rain softly blowing in from the ocean. The cars and trucks still have their lights on, despite it being 9am.

We cycle through a forest with damp trees and swampy undergrowth before coming out beside an adventure playground of hanging ropes, flying foxes and climbing walls. Is it a child's play area or a training ground for soldiers? We have our own obstacle course to contend with as I splash through a puddle and drench my legs. Merde!

The path takes us through a suburb of new houses built on cul-de-sacs, as if the town-planners were determined to discourage non-residents from entering each street. In the new world of suburbia, we all want to be King or Queen. Craig and I look into the back gardens of each house and I'm a little disturbed to see the French rural habit of a vegetable garden is not pursued in this holiday location. A clothes line, a child's swing, a deflated football and one lonely stunted palm tree does not a garden make.

Craig and I are searching for Lake Arcachon. We know it's somewhere nearby, but no matter how many roads we travel down, each ends in a T-junction. Left or right? I'm happy to forgo the search and just start cycling inland towards the Canal de Garonne, but Craig is determined to begin the journey at the Atlantic Ocean, as first planned. Even though I tell him the Lake is not really the ocean, he refuses to budge. He wants to see the water before heading east. If he's carrying me seven hundred kilometres, he wants to enjoy the symbolism of beginning in the correct location.

So we trundle along numerous back roads including one that eventually leads us to a sandy track of mud and cold puddles. A young woman walks in the opposite direction. I ask her, in faltering French, which way to the Lake. She points from where she has come and walks off, quickly. Who would want to go to the Lake in this weather? On a bike?

Finally, we arrive at the canal port where a row of dark-timber fisherman huts look bleak and untidy, with nets bundled in a heap beside each door. I lean Craig against a rock wall and, amid great ceremony, snap his photo with the lake in the background. The mist blows in from the ocean and stranded fishing boats tilt awkwardly in the mud at low tide. A black circular tube, a metre in diameter, protrudes two hundred metres into the bay. The bay itself is a horizon of mist and mud.

At least Craig is satisfied. I don't want to admit it, but I'm also chuffed to be standing, in the rain, at a western extremity of France. The water I can just see through the mist is connected to the Atlantic Ocean. The next great expanse of water I hope to see is the Mediterranean in a few weeks time. I gaze out across the lake and whisper 'bonne route' to myself.

Craig and I ride back into the holiday suburbs and promptly get lost. We're searching for a bicycle sign directing us to the town of Mios where the dedicated cycle path begins. I have the distinct impression we're going around in a huge circle. It continues to rain and my Garmin tells me we've clocked up twenty kilometres. At one point, after crossing a narrow bridge and looping left, I look below us and see the path we've just cycled on. We are going in circles!

I stop in the driveway of a bungalow. A handsome young man is unloading the boot of his car. I call out, 'Excusez-moi, ou est Mios?' He slowly walks towards me and points a lazy arm in the direction I was travelling. He smiles and says, 'Tout droit, quatre kilometre.' It's that easy. He is a *very* handsome man. Craig and I cycle off with renewed vigour and join a lovely road through a quiet forest of pines and ferns, with water seemingly leaking from the undergrowth. Everything is saturated. The ditches along the road are full of pine-tinged water. It looks good enough to drink.

We cross a bridge over the rushing l'Eyre River and cycle the main street where I park Craig outside a boulangerie. Every time I step into a French cake shop, I become a blithering zombie, ghoulishly staring at the array of pastries on offer. I attempt to smile at the woman behind the counter but it comes out all dribbly and perverted, like I have a cake fetish. Which I do. This morning, I choose a kouigh-amann, a Breton masterpiece of butter and dough that is both crusty and delicate. I take it outside to eat in front of Craig. He forgives me my sins.

I brush the crumbs from his seat and we ride awkwardly down the road to join the Mios to Bazas cycle path, created from a disused railway line. It runs for eighty kilometres, predominantly straight and level through villages and forests. At last, I can let Craig loose and we can travel unimpeded by traffic and nervous pedestrians.

I rest one hand lightly on the handlebars and admire the cannonball straight, two-metre wide tarmac in front of me. Bliss. Even with the rain continuing to fall.

'Pah, rain cannot dampen our spirits, Craig!' I call to the wind.

Craig answers by reaching 30 kph.

'Whoa, boy,' I call.

A jogger in front wonders who the hell I'm talking to. We race past him and contemplate what to have for lunch.

At Salle, I cycle past the old railway station, a double-storey building that is now somebody's maison. The name of the station is chiselled in stone above the front door. Yellow curtains drape the windows and a child's scooter on the verandah awaits a rider. I'm always secretly pleased when public buildings are turned into houses. Much better than demolition. What child wouldn't want to live in an ancient train station?

Ahead of me, a posse of school children on bicycles are being lead in single formation down the path by a balding teacher wearing a white t-shirt and fawn trousers. He has old-fashioned clips to stop his pants billowing in the breeze. As we pass, he calls out to me. I don't understand, but imagine he's just wishing me a pleasant journey and suggesting I keep right so as to not collide with any of his proteges. I call back, 'Oui!'

At the next intersection, a sign reads *route inonde, 3000 metres.* I stop and stare at the sign, wondering what to do. I decide to continue along the path for three kilometres to see just how badly the route is flooded. Perhaps I can tentatively cycle through? I consult my Garmin each kilometre and scan the path ahead. No sign of flooding. Merci!

I go back to talking to myself. Pardon. Talking to Craig. He listens in silence. After five kilometres, we come to a clearing with a picnic table and bench seat. A sandy track leads off into the forest. Opposite is a high wire fence and the roar of vehicles racing past. We have reached a major road. The cycle path turns sharp right and descends to an underpass… that is flooded with very deep water. I cover Craig's ears and scream obscenities into the rain. The dull roar of traffic ignores me. I ride down to the river. The path disappears under brown fast-flowing water. There is no way I can cycle through this.

I have no option but to sheepishly turn around and go back for five rain-soaked kilometres. Unless that bush track leads me to the D3, surely somewhere to the north? Craig and I hesitate. Sandy path or five kilometres extra cycling, in the rain? We choose the overgrown sandy path. In twenty metres we become bogged. I get off and push Craig for a few metres before jumping back in the saddle and pedalling furiously through the sand. I do this for a kilometre until I have no idea where I am. I'm breathing heavily and am angry at myself for thinking I could just magically find the road. The silence of the bush is a stark reminder of my stupidity.

Sluggishly, I turn around and return to the picnic table and cycle path, and from there back to Salle. When I eventually arrive at the intersection with the D3, it dawns on me that the teacher was warning me to take the road, not the cycle path. Bless him. And damn my limited French!

I cycle the D3, accompanied by logging trucks, delivery vans and speeding Audis. The road winds through forest and the occasional cleared field of sawn-off stumps with a pile of logs stacked high. After an hour, I arrive at the village of Housten where I locate the cycle path again. A sign points back to Salle, telling me it's an easy twelve kilometres. I've ridden twenty on the highway. I look for a sign warning of *route indonne*. There is none.

It's past lunchtime and I have no idea how many more kilometres

I have to go to reach Langon. Housten slumbers in the rain. No matter. Craig and I have a perfectly smooth wide path to cruise along.

I wonder where Cathie is and if she's found an obliging farmhouse B&B?

I wonder if there's a restaurant in the next town?

I wonder if they'll serve a bedraggled cyclist at 2pm on a Monday afternoon?

I wonder when the trains stopped running?

I wonder why the rain won't cease?

Craig wonders why I'm talking to myself...

Saint Symphorien is a beautiful village with an old stone church, its door open wide as if welcoming wet cyclists and other pilgrims. A group of townsfolk are congregating outside the hall next door, under a makeshift marquee. It looks like a Monday meeting is morphing into a party. I'm too late for the boulangerie, which closed an hour ago.

However, there is a restaurant in the town square. I park Craig under an awning, remove my grubby shoe covers, draping them over the panniers before tentatively stepping inside. An elegant woman in a white chiffon top and cream trousers, her hair swept back in a severe bun, greets me. To her credit, she appears not to notice the puddle I'm making at the entrance. She offers me a table in the centre of the restaurant. I gratefully accept and hang my jacket on the rack beside a long red leather coat.

The three-course menu is a ridiculously cheap 12.50 Euros and consists of a seafood salad starter. Merci, Madam. It's delicious, tart and sweet at the same time and washed down with a quarter-litre of house rosé, comprix. For main course, I choose cous cous with... something? I'm afraid my skill at reading French menus is limited. It turns out to be chicken, a stringy but tasty hunk of beef and a pork sausage in a stew, with vegetables. The only way to describe it is as a meat bouillabaisse. I ladle large spoons of the sauce over my cous

cous and savour the fatty goodness of the meat. If only Craig could join me. For dessert, I have strawberries and ice cream. All thoughts of getting lost, flooded paths and incessant rain have disappeared, along with the pichet de rosé.

Leaving a suitable tip and multiple *mercis* to my friendly host, I rejoin Craig and the wet path. I have ridden eighty-five kilometres. The rain drifts along with the afternoon. My thoughts turn to my beautiful wife and whether she'll enjoy cycling in the rain each day. Will she too become so involved in the trail that she starts talking to Jenny?

As if by magic, around the next corner, Cathie appears in the car.

She waves as she sloshes past before executing a quick u-turn at the T-junction and meeting me where the cycle path joins the road.

'I was getting worried,' she says.

'Nah, just cruising. No drama,' I feign indifference.

She raises a quizzical eyebrow.

'It's late in the afternoon and you still have thirty-five kilometres to go,' she says, before adding, 'You could throw Craig in the back and be dry in half-an-hour.'

I've already cycled eighty-five kilometres in the rain.

'What's eighty-five and thirty-five?' I ask.

'Too far, too many hours and too much rain,' Cathie answers.

Dear Reader. Would you think poorly of me if I allowed sad wet Craig a respite from the conditions?

I thought so.

The rain does not let up, all the way to Preignac.

Cathie has found a gorgeous chateau in a vineyard. I trundle down the driveway, relieved and exhausted. The chateau owner, Michel, a tall blond handsome man who drives a sporty Mini and wears white trousers and a pale blue shirt welcomes me with a glass of the local sauvignon blanc. I sit in the elegant but faded drawing room, two cases of sauvignon stacked in the corner and a tall gold-embossed mirror hanging over the fireplace. The smiling lycra-wearing fool gratefully accepts another glass of wine.

Our bedroom has a view over the garden and swimming pool to the estate vineyard, with two full-length opening windows and a royal red high-backed chair to sit in and wonder whether my budget can afford such an opulent lifestyle. The answer, of course, is no. But, a celebration is in order to start our journey. For one night, everyone should have a chateau to call their own. Besides, it's a modest affair with creaky floorboards, fading curtains and an old wooden wardrobe that has seen better eras. It lacks pretentiousness and that suits me fine.

Accommodation: Chateau des Grandes Vignes, 2 Les Grandes Vignes, Preignac. Friendly host, glass of wine on arrival, lovely rooms with high ceilings and ornate, if faded, furnishings. Swimming pool, vineyards and wifi. Dinner provided, if requested. Double room E85, breakfast included. My score: 17/20.

Restaurant: Michel offers a three course meal, plus a glass of wine, for E25. We have a salad for starters, followed by canard de confit with rice and vegetables and a chocolate mousse for dessert. We share the meal with a couple from Paris who tell us an extraordinary story of meeting and falling in love while working together for a large Danish company in France. When they informed the company that they were romantically involved, the woman was sacked within a fortnight and the man soon after. The company even cited their romance as one of the prime reasons for their dismissal. They both sued and won compensation. Love survives despite corporate madness! My score: 14/20 (for the meal) 0/20 (for a certain Danish company and their work practices)

Route Tips: The Mios to Bazas cycle path is a wonderful utilisation of an old railway line. While it's sad to see public transport infrastructure dismantled, it's pleasing that the route has been maintained for cyclists and walkers and birdwatchers. A gem of a path. Highly recommended, particularly for families and children, away from the dangers of motor vehicles. Watch for signs with the words *route inondee*.

Distance cycled: 120 km

Actual distance (without the detours and getting lost): 98 km

What I should have said: 'Monsieur, did you say *inondee*? What is *inondee*?'

Chapter Two

Preignac to Sainte-Bazeille

I pull back the curtains of our bedroom window and look over the vineyards. In the distance, a tractor starts and a dog jumps onto the seat beside the driver. Birds sing, the sun peeks behind high cloud and today is Cathie's first day of long-distance cycling. I advise a large breakfast.

Michel obliges with cheese, ham, baguettes, croissants and an array of confiture. We farewell the car, parked discreetly next to a hedge, before cycling out the front gate and heading south towards the Mediterranean.

First stop?

Two kilometres along the road, to adjust the panniers on Jenny. It seems as if she's complaining about her load and one pannier keeps popping out. I tighten nuts and bolts with an Allen key as if I know what I'm doing before we start again. Forward!

In Langon, we cycle across the bridge over the Garonne. The river is flood green and flowing swiftly, carrying branches and debris downstream. We take minor roads keeping as close as possible to the left bank. Cathie and Jenny are acquitting themselves admirably. She leads, I follow all the way to Saint Macaire, a Cite Medieval blessed with the beautiful 12th century Eglise Saint Sauveur which has a wonderfully evocative ochre-coloured mural above the single nave. Curiously, there are two cherubs reclining along one side wall of the church at floor level. One is headless. I scan the rest of the interior, expecting to locate the cherub head, perhaps decoratively lodged above one of the Stations of the Cross. But the mystery remains.

From the remparts, we have a view of the Garonne rampaging below. Given recent experience, I wonder if the cycle path will be *inondee* ahead?

We stop for a coffee in the village square. The cafe has music posters on the wall, jazz honking from the speakers and a waiter with a goatee and a stylish hat. I've stepped from the 12th century into 1957. Unfortunately, as with many French cafes, the coffee is not up to standard. The French, bless them, can do everything well, except coffee. With food, cars, wine, architecture and lifestyle, they succeed brilliantly and with great innovation. But alas, they use robusta beans, not the better-quality arabica to make their steaming brew and it tastes like fine Garonne mud. On the plus side, it only costs one Euro and there's a sucre cube nearby to lessen the impact.

No more talk of bad coffee.

We cycle the morning along back roads and beside vineyards and neat rows of trees. Under a green canopy is a gypsy camp, a half-circle of caravans with smoke rising from a smouldering log. A man sits on a plastic chair in front of a caravan. He wears a black hat and leans back casually, his legs extended. He is sleeping.

We cross the river at Castets-en-Dorthe, where the Canal de Garonne begins. At the port, where the canal joins the river, four cyclists are taking turns at being photographed with the lock master who is dressed in blue overalls. He seems bemused at all the attention and happily poses with each cyclist. They have either finished their journey, or like us, are just beginning. The two men are dressed in cycling gear while their female partners wear more relaxed shorts and tops. They laugh and joke with the lock master as we begin our two hundred kilometre friendship with the canal.

The Canal de Garonne dates from the 19th century and connects Castets with Toulouse and subsequently, its more famous sister, the Canal du Midi. Together, the Canal des Deux Mers allowed vessels to transport goods from the Atlantic to the Mediterranean, if the Garonne River co-operated by not being in flood, of course.

Like the Canal du Midi, the Garonne has thousands of elegant plane trees lining its banks. They provide shade and a certain romantic timelessness to the canals. Sadly, they are under threat from a wilt infection that was only discovered in 2006, although it was brought to Europe unwittingly by American soldiers during World War Two. The fungus will force the authorities to fell all forty-two thousand trees before they die and their branches fall on hapless cyclists and walkers.

I'll repeat that. Forty-two thousand trees. It beggars belief.

Within a few kilometres of joining the canal path, we see a tree with an orange dot painted on its trunk. I look up. Instead of a canopy of green, this tree has a paltry few brown leaves and skeleton branches. It is slated for the chop. The plane trees are planted very closely together, so for the time being, perhaps the culling of some trees will not be noticed. But, eventually...

The authorities, aware of the iconic status of these trees, are planting new ones which will be immune to the wilt infection. We cycle slowly under the umbrella of green and marvel at the quietness and shade they offer. We're in a cocoon. The sound of the outside world seems muted and far away.

At regular intervals, we pass under single arch concrete bridges that span the canal. They are simple and functional and provide a lovely frame for the rows of plane trees ahead. Each bridge signals a possible detour to a village beside the waterway. We can't resist following one of these narrow roads on the left bank and soon become hopelessly lost.

Cue three kilometres of cycling in a circle before we discover a D road that leads us across an elegant bridge designed by Gustave Eiffel, he of a certain Paris tower. When he designed this bridge, Eiffel was a humble public servant, but this artifice bears the unmistakable stamp of the master. Not even the wonders of Eiffel can stop the rain from tumbling down as we cycle across the bridge and into La Reole. We climb the cobblestone streets of the old town and stop at the first open restaurant, slinking inside and quickly removing our shoe covers and jackets before the waitress appears. After hanging our jackets on the rack, we wait to be shown to a table.

Three teenage girls appear to be the only workers. The tall girl with long brown hair, an open face and nervous smile approaches. I ask for a table. She looks at me without answering, then rushes into the kitchen. Is my French that bad? Did I inadvertently say something obscene? A very flustered man comes from the kitchen and hurriedly shows us to a table. The restaurant is full with lunch groups.

The man disappears into the kitchen. We wait for a menu. The three girls stand behind the counter and look hopefully into the kitchen through the serving area. The man, who turns out to be the chef, places four plates of confit de canard on the serving bench and the girls carry them nervously to the table of businessmen under the glass ceiling at the rear of the restaurant. They giggle as they return to their station behind the counter.

Each girl tries not to meet the eyes of the other diners. A couple opposite us look awkwardly around, hoping for service. It's apparent that the chef has brought his daughter and her two friends into work today for the experience. Or because his usual waitress is ill.

I say 'excusez-moi' in a loud voice and the shorter girl in jeans and blue top, who looks a little like the chef comes over to our table. I point to the menu on the bench and she offers one between Cathie and I. Before she has time to leave, we both order the formule menu which consists of two courses, a fish soup for entree and confit de canard for main course. And a glass of rosé. All for ten Euros. Great value, if the chef can cook it all himself and get one of the girls to bring it to us.

Inspired by my forthrightness, the couple at the nearby table call one of the girls and place their order as well. The girl rushes back to the kitchen to tell her Dad about the mutiny in the restaurant. She stays in there to help him dish up the soup. The third teenager, a French-African girl with wild hair and a nervous grin brings us the bowls of soup. Before she leaves, I ask for bread, s'il vous plait. Suddenly, the restaurant seems to be functioning.

The soup is delicious.

The man from the nearby table catches my attention and winks. A pattern is set. The three girls stay behind the counter until called by a diner, or directed to do something by the chef. It seems to work for everyone concerned. When we finish our soup, I raise my hand and the tall, open-faced girl immediately removes our bowls. The chef's daughter smiles.

Soon after, Cathie and I are enjoying an excellent confit, the skin of the duck crisp and salty, the flesh cooked to perfection. Under tremendous pressure, the lone chef is performing miracles. It's all running smoothly until one of the businessman orders a coffee. The French-African girl returns to the counter, holding her hands in the air as if to say, 'pour quoi!'

No-one knows how to operate the espresso machine.

The chef's daughter bites her lip and looks hopefully into the kitchen. Her father is in the middle of cooking the duck. I'm about to get up and offer my services when the chef places two duck dishes on the counter and sees the look of anguish on his daughter's face. She whispers a single word to him, 'cafe.' He wipes his hands on the apron and comes out to the machine. The businessman will get his caffeine.

I'd love to stay and see Part Two of *le chef et le adolescents*, but the rain has stopped. I don't bother asking for the bill, just offering a E20 note to the chef on the way out. We leave a tip on the table. The girls smile, the daughter permits herself a friendly wave and we leave, feeling satisfied we have helped the restaurant trade in La Reole, in a small way.

Back on the path, a woman wearing a t-shirt and billowing trousers rides towards me shouting at the top of her voice. I keep to the side of the path and smile, saying 'Bonjour.' She answers by yelling, 'Merci pour bonjour, merci pour bonjour,' as we pass. The afternoon unwinds like a mad woman on a bicycle.

We stop at the 11th century chapel at Tersac, leaving Craig and

Jenny beside the fence, before quietly opening the gate and wandering through the cemetery surrounding the church. The first grave I see is of a child who died in 1911, at the age of twenty-three months. The small cross is dwarfed by the imposing graves of soldiers killed in the First World War. The entrance to the church is sheltered by a wide portico with a moss-covered tile roof. The door is locked. It's a peaceful place, looking down on the still waters of the canal.

We have booked a B&B at Sainte-Bazeille, a few kilometres east of the canal. As is usual with me, I've written down the address but not paid much attention to the directions from the canal.

The entrance to Sainte-Bazeille, like in so many French towns, is along an avenue of stately trees. The corridor of green always puts me in a happy mood, as if they've planted them just for me.

'There should me a sign for the B&B in the village,' I tell Cathie.

Did she just roll her eyes?

Sure enough, no signs.

'I think the directions said something about Jurques Nord,' I say, hopefully.

'Jerks,' Cathie replies.

'Jurques, with a Q,' I add, 'and, yes, I should have written down proper directions.'

I ask a gentleman washing his car if he knows where Jurques Nord is? He turns off the hose and calls to his wife through the window. She goes on the internet and looks. The man smiles as we wait for Google authority.

Non.

No Jurques Nord.

We ride back into the village and I enter the Mairie. Surely the town authorities will know? The woman at the front desk consults the huge district map on the wall. Non. She reverts to Google, with the same result as the previous encounter. I'm hugely impressed with the friendliness of everybody as they try to find a Jurques for the jerk. Eventually, after consulting everyone in the office, someone vaguely remembers there is a Liet called Jurques east of the village. I am given directions, more in hope than certainty.

I feign confidence as I rejoin Cathie waiting patiently outside with a bewildered Craig and Jenny.

'No worries,' I say, 'We ride east.' I point straight ahead.

'That's north,' Cathie says.

'Yep, we go east, then north,' I answer.

We trundle past an ecole and a rue commemorating the life of a teenage poet, Sabine Sicaud who lived between 1913 and 1928.

Miraculously, we see a sign for Jurques.

'Just along here,' I say, my voice tinged with false authority.

Sure enough, we come to a major D road, with cars speeding past. We both stop. It's hopeless. I don't know what to do. Cathie smiles and points to a sign opposite. The B&B is just up that narrow C road.

When we finally arrive, the owner welcomes us with a coffee before going back to knitting in the jardin. Madam and her husband keep ducks and sheep and have a tree in the backyard full of ripe cherries. I ask permission. She nods readily.

'Pour confiture,' she says.

I spend a quiet afternoon sitting on a ladder, eating cherries, talking to the sheep. Cathie goes on the internet and writes down detailed directions to our accommodation tomorrow night. Just in case.

Accommodation: Chambres d'Hotes du Clos Semper Felix, Liue-dit Jurques Nord, Sainte-Bazeille. Lovely rural property, friendly hosts (who drove us to dinner and picked us up afterwards), swimming pool, wifi, excellent breakfast. Double room E65, breakfast included. My score: 17/20.

Restaurant: La Payung Chez Alice, Sainte-Bazeille. Just out of town on the main road, heading towards the SuperU, is a garden display village, with Indonesian thatched roof huts and sculptures of Buddhas. At night, it becomes a delightful setting for dinner. One of the owners speaks English and she lets us choose our table. Her eight-year-old daughter does homework near the bar, watched by the husband, a gentle giant with tattoos and a shaven head. He is the chef. We order the formule menu for E13, which comes with 500 mls of rosé. We serve ourselves from the buffet for entree. For main, I have two huge pieces of beef, flame cooked over the barbecue with salad and frites. The meat is delicious. Dessert is home made chocolate mousse. After dinner, the daughter leads us both to the ornamental pond to see if we can find the two huge black fish that lurk in the depths. We walk across a bridge to a thatched hut built on the pond and lean over the side, searching. The girl points, gleefully, 'Noir!' The chef comes over to join in with his daughter's celebration.

Good value, simple food, lovely hosts, wonderful location in good weather. My score: 17/20.

Distance cycled today: 68 km

Actual distance: 52 km

What I should have said: 'Monsieur, I am happy to be the waiter for your fine establishment!'

Chapter Three

Sainte-Bazeille to Nerac

Over a delicious breakfast including fruit compote and home made confiture, we thank Madam once again for driving us to the restaurant and picking us up afterwards. She smiles and offers me another croissant. I can hardly refuse.

The morning is overcast but warm as we cycle back through the tree-lined entrance to Sainte-Bazeille to rejoin the canal path. As we cross the bridge over the Garonne, a deer scampers from the undergrowth and bounds across the field beside the river. Surely that's a good omen for the day.

At Fourques-sur-Garonne, surrounded by streets of modern uniform houses, a small Mairie and an ecole, sits a squat round-ended church with a statue of Madonna on the roof, facing the canal and the river rather than her usual position attending the Cross at the front of the church. She watches the river to 'protege les population des caprices et des crues de la riviere.' To protect the population against the changing moods of the river.

We ride on top of the levee for the morning, the path alternates between hard packed clay and tarmac. A few joggers sweat alongside the peaceful canal, a woman walks her dog who stops every few metres to sniff and two men work on converting an old barn into a maison atop a rise on the opposite bank. When finished, they will have a serene view of the waterway and surrounding fields.

We cross another concrete arched bridge and ride up a steep hill into Le Mas d'Agenais, which has a delightful spring-fed lavoir near the canal. The house opposite the lavoir is a riot of flowering blossoms as if the spring has blessed the owners with endless colour and bloom.

Le Mas has an ancient covered market built of sturdy wooden beams in the square next to a church that, astonishingly, has a

Rembrandt painting on permanent display. We can't resist a look, stepping into the cool interior of the 12th century Saint Vincent church. At first, we don't see the Rembrandt and spend a lively few minutes debating whether the painting of Christ and his disciples in front of us is really the Master's work.

'It looks a little... modern,' I venture.

'It's bloody awful,' says my more artistic wife.

'Maybe it was his blue period,' I suggest.

'That was Picasso,' Cathie says.

'Oh.'

We stroll the interior and, sure enough, in the next aisle is the true Rembrandt, a very dark and bleak Christ on the Cross, almost 3-D in its depiction of the saviour's visage. It's perhaps not his most expressive work, but I'm still amazed that it's here, unguarded, in such a small village. I could reach up and lift...

'Don't even think about it,' whispers Cathie.

Instead of the art heist of the century, we go to the boulangerie and buy the best canelle I've ever eaten. Crisp and caramelised on the outside, moist and custardy on the inside. Two masterpieces in the one village!

Back on the canal, the plane trees give way to open fields of wheat on our left, creeper and a twenty-metre high bank to our right. We cruise along slowly. I know we're both thinking of lunch. The rhythm of the journey is established. Eating and drinking, followed by thinking of eating and drinking and guilty calculations on how far we have to cycle to burn off all those calories.

Damazan is a feudal village founded in the 13th century on a hill, above an attractive port on the canal. We circle the village before deciding on La Penia Restaurant, enticed by the numerous tables on the verandah shaded by vines. Unfortunately, every outside table is reserved. We make do with a position near the entrance and eat a three-course lunch, perfectly suited to workmen and cyclists. Sure enough, by the time we leave, every outdoor table is packed with men in overalls and big boots. In the car park are eight vans and two trucks. The way to choose a good restaurant in a French village? Look for vans in the car park. It works every time.

The half-litre of rosé over lunch slows us down in the sleepy afternoon. Cathie leads and directs us to turn off the canal eleven kilometres from our destination for the evening which is Nerac, a royal town, on a hill west of the canal. I have visions of getting lost again, just like yesterday.

The D road is quiet and within a few kilometres we come to Vianne, a magnificent Bastide town surrounded by a three metre high wall, with a single arched entrance on each of the four sides. We cycle, like modern royalty through the archway and enter another world of peace and security. Barely a soul moves. A cat sleeps on a stoop and the swallows circle the guarded sky. It's not until we reach the centre square that we see another person, an old man with a walking stick, sitting on the park bench. A pizzeria is open, the flyscreen fluttering lightly in the breeze.

We ride the deserted streets and exit via the archway beside the river which is spanned by a suspension bridge. Imagine being a child living here with your very own walled town and river. It's intoxicating. We ride back into the bastide once more. It's hard to leave. An old woman works in her garden, she smiles as we cycle past.

Finally, we depart via the northern archway and rejoin the D road where the train station has been converted into a workshop for an artisan glassblower. Further along the road is a glassblowing museum which is closed, but appears to be full of lamps designed in the 1970s. Colours of garish orange, lime green and turquoise dominate. The lampshades are either mushroom-shaped or blobby extravagances inspired by too many bad acid trips. I wish the museum was open.

Nerac, which we find easily because Cathie leads, is initially a disappointment with strip shopping and service stations. This changes when we enter the old town and tentatively cycle down the steep cobblestone street where our B&B is located.

Voila! There it is.

I stride confidently to the front door and knock. No answer. I press the bell. Still no answer. One more loud knock. Non.

Cathie hands me the phone number of the B&B. She has thought of everything. I ring and when a woman answers, try to explain in bad French that we are here, repeating, 'Ici, l'hotel,' over and over. She does not understand. She hands the phone to someone who speaks a little English.

'Ici, l'hotel,' I repeat.

The woman says, 'You are at the hotel?'

'Oui,' I say.

'What hotel,' she asks.

'Ici,' I plead in frustration.

Suddenly the door opens and I'm looking at a woman holding a phone. We both hang up. She says, 'You said you were at the hotel.'

'Yes, this hotel,' I say.

She laughs, 'This is not a hotel, this is a chambre d'hote.'

I'm tempted to suggest this nonsensical conversation would not be necessary if the doorbell functioned properly. She introduces us to the owner, the original voice on the telephone. She is reminiscent of everyone's favourite Aunt with wispy grey hair, glasses and a light blue cardigan and plaid skirt. She leads us around the corner, unlocking large wooden doors and we enter a sunny courtyard at the back of the house. Incongruously, there is a twenty-metre high stone tower in the garden, adjoining the maison. It looks very old.

In the evening, our French Auntie offers us an aperitif of armagnac, a strong brandy unique to this region. We are joined by a middle-aged man named Phillipe, who wears spectacles and an open-necked shirt. He speaks excellent English and explains he's a chef who is staying here for a week in his job as Chief Examiner for a cooking school. We sit in the garden and, between sips, I look up at the tower.

'Vous voulez voir?' our host asks.

'Oui, Merci,' I say, standing immediately, before she changes her mind.

She leads us into the tower. The temperature cools immediately as we climb the circular stairs. Phillipe joins us and gallantly acts as translator. Madam tells a long involved story of the town and its relationship to Henry IV and his renowned lust for women. She laughs discreetly as she says this. She explains the Catholic/Protestant divide that Henry IV had to straddle, along with his extravagant desires. I get the impression that Phillipe is censoring much of what our host is saying. Even so, Henry IV sounds like he was a party King. The tower dates from the early 16th century and the circular top floor contains a double bed and a fantastic view over the town. We wonder who is staying here tonight?

Phillipe shakes his head. Not him.

Not us. Our room is on the ground floor of the main house and has a double bed with a simple pillow roll, a bed cover, a wooden wardrobe, and in the bathroom a double window that opens out to a garden of sorts. This afternoon we washed our clothes and hung them in the walled garden, just above the street. It's homely and plain, just like everyone's Aunt.

'Pour extraordinaire...' she says.

Aren't we extraordinary enough, I think.

In the evening, we wander up to the Notre Dame church, which has a circular lead light window above the organ, depicting Mary cradling a dying Jesus, while twelve Marys, one for each clock hand, are in a state of solemn reflection. The church is narrow and tall, with an elevated vaulted ceiling. From Notre Dame, we walk down to the old town and along the river where a busload of tourists are boarding a barge for an evening cruise. There are three hotels, each with a restaurant, beside the river. We choose the one with outdoor tables, next to the old bridge. It's called, predictably Cafe Pont Vieux. A few minutes after we've ordered, we see Phillipe crossing the bridge. We wave to him and he readily joins us for dinner. I've never eaten with a chef before. I wonder if he'll critically analyse each dish?

The short answer is no. Phillipe ignores the formule menu and orders magret du canard. He eats slowly and tells us all about his job, his love of food, his desire to produce the best with the ingredients available to him. He is a well-travelled and erudite dinner companion. He even takes my joke about French coffee in his stride.

'We try to save money, perhaps with... lesser beans,' he explains.

'But, in the kitchen, the French use only the best,' I suggest.

He smiles, astutely, 'No, we *make* the best, from what we have.'

Accommodation: Chambre d'hotes La Tour de Brazalem, 3 rue de l'Ecole, Nerac. A welcoming and friendly, if rather forgetful host, simple rooms, quiet courtyard and excellent location in the old town. Ask for the room in the tower! Double room E55, breakfast included. My score: 14/20.

Restaurant: Auberge du Pont Vieux, 19 rue Sederie, Nerac. A lovely location beside the river and the old bridge. We had a three-course formule menu which consisted of chevre chaud salad for starter, faux fillet of beef with potato gratin and beans for main course and the obligatory crème brûlée for dessert. It was excellent value in a romantic setting with the ducks gliding along the river (when not on somebody's plate!) and the swallows swooping along the surface of the water. My score: 16/20

Route tips: I strongly recommend a detour to Vianne and Nerac, two beautiful towns on the River Baise.

Distance cycled: 67 km

Actual distance: 58 km

What I should have said: 'But, Madam, we *are* special, extraordinary, worthy of the tower!'

Chapter Four

Nerac to Saint-Nicolas-de-la-Grave

The day begins with breakfast in the garden, earlier than all the other guests. The French are late risers and our host, the kindly Aunt, has bent the rules to allow us an early start. She pours herself a large bowl of coffee as compensation for being up with the birds and the Australians.

After checking out, we ride slowly over the cobblestone old bridge and once more admire the uniform colours of the buildings.

'I'd call it dusty beige,' I suggest.

'Wet sandstone,' says Cathie.

'Rusted wheat,' I counter.

'We sound like a Dulux colour chart,' says Cathie.

Soon after, we encounter our first hill and both stop thinking of paint schemes. The sun is blazing hot already and one of us forgot to fill his water bottle. Craig and Jenny are both developing squeaks. Craig complains loudly and regularly.

We have sweeping views of the countryside around Nerac as we climb. Rolling fields of wheat, reminiscent in colour to the Nerac old town are patterned by narrow country lanes. On a distant hill, a white church stands regally. Near Espriens, I stop beside a closed mechanics workshop. Underneath an old Renault van, jacked up on blocks, is a metal container full of sump oil and rainwater. I lean Craig against the tin shed and dip my finger into the concoction. I figure there's enough oil amongst the rainwater to keep Craig happy. Using an old rag, I rub his chain with the mixture. He'll either quieten down or rust, I imagine.

Craig just keeps creaking. After a long easy downhill, it's back to climbing and I look behind hopefully for my wife. These are her first serious climbs of the journey. I wait on the crest of a hill. It's a beautiful day and the views are truly majestic. I count four church spires, one for each neighbouring village. Cathie puffs up the hill and zips down the other side after a cursory smile.

Outside of Bruch, we stop at a roadside cherry tree and eat the ripe fruit, tart and juicy. In the village, an old lady carrying a brown leather handbag over her wrist, watches a Council worker with a chainsaw cut down a small tree in the square. He does his best to ignore her as she walks closer. But on this quiet street, there are only the two of them and we cyclists. Eventually, he turns off the chainsaw and is given, I imagine, a lecture on removing shade and beauty from the town square. He listens, his eyes downcast. He shrugs his shoulders as if to say, 'I am just a Council employee.' The woman walks off. The worker lights a cigarette and waits until she's out of hearing before starting the chainsaw. We refill our water bottles and go looking for a certain canal.

Unexpectedly, there are no plane trees on the canal. I wonder if the chainsaw brigade has been through here. It's getting hotter by the minute and I contemplate the perfect cycling speed to generate a cooling breeze.

The result?

Anything under 14 kph is too slow, and over 22 kph is too much effort for no greater reward. We cruise along at a sensible 16 kph.

Beside the canal grow seemingly endless orchards of plums, some covered in nets, others left open to the sun and birds. On the far bank, a clutter of creeper winds its way along the path while on this side, we have the hard gravel track to ourselves. At Serignac-sur-Garonne, the church has a curious coiled spire, seemingly twisting its way upwards. It's a sleepy village. We'd hoped for a boulangerie.

Onwards to Agen, the prune capital of France, recently voted the 'most liveable city in the Republic.' It's an imposing entrance over a majestic canal bridge, the longest in France at five hundred and eighty metres, with twenty-three arches. We glide above the Garonne River and plan a boulangerie treat in such a supposedly delightful town.

However, while crossing the bridge with limited cycle space, we both notice the walkers are giving us very little room. We're having to cycle close to the canal water, not a pleasing prospect on a bumpy surface. I'm leading and numerous times I have to apply the brakes and swerve to miss a pedestrian. They walk in rows of two and three and there's no way through. I've never encountered this rudeness before. Not in a country where the citizens are so proud of their cultured civility.

It doesn't improve once we've crossed the bridge. There's now more room, but still we're forced closer to the canal. Finally, I lose my temper and hold my line. A stout man in a white business shirt and ironed trousers walks towards me and I ride towards him. He has three metres of space to his right, I have less than a metre. He sees me a few metres away. And ignores me.

I've misjudged the space. I cannot safely swerve or I may dive into the canal. I slow down and drop my shoulder, hoping to miss him. Our arms graze each other. I cycle a few metres before stopping. Cathie pulls up behind me.

'Did you see that?' I ask.

'He just ran into me,' she says, red-faced.

'You?'

'He lifted his arm as I went past. It didn't hurt, but...'

'What the...'

I'm lost for words. Perhaps he thought I'd hit him and he was retaliating by running into my wife? Surely not.

Do I chase him and...

And what? Begin a schoolyard argument on who hit whom first?

'Forget it,' Cathie says.

I take a deep breath and feel enormous guilt. Maybe I provoked him? But, I'd tried to avoid a collision. Cathie shrugs. We cycle along the canal in confused silence, deliberately giving every walker a wide berth. They still seem to be taking up more room than necessary.

Between the canal path and the Centre Ville is a four track railway line and a noisy traffic-filled road. From a distance, the centre of Agen appears grimy and unpleasant, but perhaps that's just my present state of mind?

'You know, even though I'm hungry, I don't want to go into Agen,' Cathie says.

I know exactly how she feels. We pedal faster to put as many kilometres as possible between ourselves and France's most liveable town.

Still shaking with frustration, I stop at a bench seat a few kilometres further on. We sit in the shade and slowly eat the bag of cherries we'd saved from Bruch.

Every jogger who passes nods hello.

A long line of teenagers on bikes head towards us. The first rider is a pretty girl with long brown hair. She smiles at us and says, 'Bonjour.' We answer. The next rider also says hello and smiles. And the one after that. Everyone in the group breezes past wishing us a 'good day.' By the time the last rider, a boy with black-rimmed glasses and curly hair has past, we're both happy and smiling and have forgotten Agen and the incident with the businessman.

The sun is shining brightly and we are eating hand-picked ripe fruit beside a canal in one of the most beautiful countries on earth.

Even Craig refrains from squeaking for the next few kilometres. Or perhaps I've just learned to ignore him.

A sign ahead points to the village of Lafox and informs us that it has a boulangerie, called *Le bonheur est dans le pain*, roughly translated as *happiness is in the bread*. The sign also tells us that Lafox has a magasin de velo, which means I can finally provide Craig and Jenny with the oil they've been craving.

The waitress at *Le bonheur* is suitably chirpy as she sells us two divine croissants d'amande and she readily fills our water bottles, despite the boulangerie selling bottled water. The croissants are a glorious mixture of flaky pastry on the outside and soft ooziness inside. Satisfied, we pedal to the bike shop where a young man leads me between gleaming expensive road bikes to the accessories section where I buy a small container of chain lube. It's E5.20, but he suggests E5. It's as though everyone we meet this morning is trying to make up for the moody businessman.

Craig and Jenny revel in smooth quietness as we pedal back to the canal. We sip from full water bottles. Not even the torrid sun can daunt us. A row of plane trees shade the opposite bank where there isn't a path. I make up a song about it. Please adjust the melody as you prefer...

'We're on the wrong side of the plane trees,
the wrong side of the plane trees.
It's stinking hot here
and shady over there...
we're on the wrong side of the plane trees.'

This ditty leads us into Lamagistere, a quiet village on the Garonne River that was the scene of a major sabotage operation on a German-controlled railway line by French partisans during the Second World War. It's much more peaceful today, with only the Gare restaurant open.

We are greeted by a smiling waitress wearing a swirling loose smock and sandals. She looks more suited to the beach than this back road cafe. She shows us to a table and explains the menu in speedy French. We have no idea what's on offer, but both nod willingly when we hear the price of eleven Euros for three courses including pichet de rosé. Whenever I'm offered wine inclusive of the meal, I cannot say no. It's a Pavlovian response that I wish I could control, but free wine always wins. The meal is simple and filling, the wine light and refreshing. We both notice how the waitress easily serves a restaurant of twenty-five people, unaided. Perhaps she should run a waitress Ecole? I know three teenagers in La Reole who would enrol.

After lunch, stupefied by the vin, we lose our way again. We both forgot to make detailed directions to tonight's accommodation. We have the address but nothing else. I know our destination is on the right side of the canal and river, so confidently turn-off the path just before the left bank town of Moissac. We cycle along a lonely back road that appears to be heading in the correct direction. It's a splendid road, no cars and only crows swooping over the wheat fields beside us. I feel as though I'm pedalling through a Van Gogh painting with the strong afternoon light highlighting the colours of the landscape. Then the road narrows and becomes pot-holed.

A car approaches. I wave down the driver. The young woman explains that if we continue we will reach the river and no further. We must turn around. The directions she gives to our destination are incredibly complicated and involved.

We spend a wandering afternoon cycling between canal and river, through vineyards and across bridges before we arrive at Saint Nicolas de la Grave and, as if in sympathy, the first sign we see points us in the direction of our B&B, which is a kilometre out of town.

Our hosts are Fred and David. A Belgian and an Irishman, respectively. They immediately offer us a beer with a dash of sirup and a delicious apple cake, just baked by Fred. We sit by the pool and listen to their stories.

David is a gregarious man who speaks numerous languages and works from home for the Dale Carnegie organisation, of the 'win friends and influence people' doctrine. I'm immediately suspicious of all self-help agendas, but David brushes off my concerns with a long humorous discourse on how Mr Carnegie applied simple logic to his business relationships and built a profitable empire in the process. David is a living example of such happy positivity. His partner, Fred runs the B&B while David spends hours on skype, talking in various languages to Carnegie franchises throughout the world.

We drink more beer, eat cake and contemplate diving in the pool. How can we resist?

We've also booked a Table d'hote meal with Fred and David and the four of us are joined by Fred's Mum, who lives in the back garden in a caravan. Fred and his Mum have limited English, so David spends the night translating. Fred serves delicious food based on the philosophy that all ingredients should be in season and bought from within a one kilometre radius, where possible.

The first course is a sublime meat pie with beef from the adjoining farm and vegetables grown locally. This is followed by canard skewers, honeyed carrots and potatoes.

'Don't tell me the duck is from next door as well,' I say.

'Of course,' says David.

'And Fred killed it,' I add, in jest.

'He did, actually,' says David, smiling.

Fred nods in agreement. He's a giant of a man with broad shoulders and big hands, but he's so gentle I can't imagine him hurting anything. He speaks in rapid French.

'A group of us get together for the killing,' translates David.

I finish everything on my plate. It tastes divine and I don't want to upset Fred! His mother smiles fondly, proud of her son's considerable culinary skills. For dessert we have strawberries and Chantilly cream.

In the late evening we sit on the tiny balcony of our room and watch the sun set over the vines. We sip the last of our wine and decide to stay for two more days to explore the region more closely. David tells us there's a party in town on Saturday night. He winks and says it'll be worth the wait.

Accommodation: Douce France, Chemin d'Auvillar, Saint Nicolas de la Grave. Multi-lingual friendly hosts, swimming pool, wifi and excellent breakfast. Dinner on request. Double room E60, breakfast included. My score: 18/20.

Restaurant: Eat in with Fred and David. A three-course meal with 500 ml of wine costs E18 per person. My score: 17/20.

Distance cycled: 73 km

Actual distance cycled: 87 km

What I should have said: 'Agen? A prune is just a dried-up plum, isn't it.'

Chapter Five

Saint Nicolas de la Grave to Auvillar, return

Breakfast is tasty and plentiful, as we expected. Fred sits with us and practices his English while we torture his native language.

'Animaux de massacre, aujourd'hui,' I joke.

Fred laughs and tells us he will prepare the rooms for new guests, instead. Such a kind gentle man... in the body of a Rugby front-rower. As if on cue, David walks in.

Everyone laughs.

Fred and David are wearing exactly the same patterned check shirts. David rolls his eyes.

'I will change,' he says.

'Apres croissant chocolate,' says Fred.

David cannot resist. He plonks himself down and pours a coffee.

'Cathie and I always wear the same colours,' I say.

'Yeah, but not the same clothes!' David responds.

'I don't look good in a dress,' I admit.

The day is warm with high cloud as we pedal away from Douce France for a circular ride around the region. Our destination is the medieval village of Auvillar. David warned it was on top of a steep hill. I shrugged. We are sans panniers. Craig will treat any hill with suitable disdain.

We cycle along quiet lanes between apple orchards and vineyards. On one farm, sheep, goats and horses all lie in the thick green grass while chickens cluck around in the dirt. There are no ducks. Fred has obviously been this way. There are a few fields of newly planted corn, still saturated by the recent rains that have swollen the Garonne River. I wonder if the wheat fields will dry out enough to allow the tractors to harvest. Village talk is of the wettest year in recent memory.

Auvillar is a treat. In the old town the houses are built of rose-coloured brick, similar to the famous colours of nearby Toulouse. The locals are out in force this Saturday with the men looking very dashing. One elderly gentleman wears mustard slacks, a yellow shirt and an apricot scarf. A younger man with swept-back lacquered hair, makes do with cream trousers and a pink shirt. They both wear leather slip-on shoes.

In the circular covered market there are stalls selling bread, cheese and saucisson.

Just off the main square is the vine-covered La Baladin restaurant with a flowering garden and shady verandahs. It's so appealing we can't resist. We walk inside where the wacky interior features old-fashioned hats and wooden chairs hanging from the walls and a table attached to the ceiling. We take our place at a more logically-positioned table and are served delicious inexpensive galettes by a young man who dresses more plainly than his contemporaries.

Ever since visiting Brittany a few years ago, I've been a sucker for the galette and cider combination. How can you go wrong with jambon, fromage and a runny oeuf. This galette is exceptional with oozy cheese and smokey ham. It's like a second breakfast, washed down with alcohol. Tres bon!

After lunch, we wander the cobblestone streets. Many buildings in the square are decorated with modern sculptures of what appear to be leprechauns. Perhaps David's Irish influence has stretched all the way here? It's a curious and humorous addition to what was recently voted 'one of France's most beautiful villages.' The view from outside the Church of St Peter's confirms this, with the Garonne flowing wildly below. It comes as no surprise to learn this is a stop on the pilgrim route to Santiago de Compostela. The pilgrims always choose wisely.

We cycle slowly uphill and west from Auvillar into the wheat-field countryside of rolling hills dotted with clumps of forest. We pass a woman loaded down with a backpack and camping gear as she walks along the dirt shoulder. She waves cheerily, such is the optimism of the pilgrims. At Bardigues, there's a newly-cropped row of plane trees announcing the village entry. It looks sleepy and silent this Saturday until we turn a corner and see scores of diners in a restaurant with a commanding view of the landscape. It's a riot of colour, from glasses of rosé to the aforementioned apricot scarves and mustard trousers. The women wear the more discreet shades of beige or cream.

Cathie and I in basic black lycra, cruise downhill and along a narrow road on the side of a rise with a view of a bubbling stream below. Old farm houses dot the landscape, birds serenade the afternoon and in the next village of St Michel we eat a delayed second course of ripe cherries from a tree beside the road. It's very difficult not to recline in the shade and fall asleep. Instead, we plough on over gentle hills until we reach Saint Nicolas de la Grave from the south side. There's one cafe open, ringed by a posse of leather-clad motorcyclists drinking beer. We sit at a nearby table and order a coffee.

In the town square opposite, a group of men set up long rows of tables and chairs for tonight's event. By the look of things, they're expecting the whole town to attend.

We cycle home, slowly. In the afternoon I fall asleep beside the pool. Cathie tells me I snored, but only a little.

A few hours later, we return to the town square to see it transformed with hundreds of people gathered at the tables, lights strung from the trees and a band on stage playing very loud rock music. For ten Euro, we buy a three-course dinner of pate de campagne, magret de canard and a choice of desserts. Biere pression is two Euro and a one-litre bottle of the local red wine is four Euro. Not long after finishing my meal, the organiser of the event comes around selling raffle tickets. A stout woman with a ready smile, she is followed by a man holding a very large leg of ham. For one Euro, I can attempt to guess the exact weight of the jambon. The winner takes home the ham, of course.

Surprise of the evening is the second band. Three men and one woman come on stage and begin playing jaunty rollicking Irish music. David winks at me across the table. He's in his element. The singer who I'm told speaks only French, sings the English-language tunes with a perfect Irish lilt. David cannot find fault with his elocution. He's devilishly handsome as well.

The audience range in age from the five year olds playing football behind the kitchen to an elegant woman sitting one table away, who is rumoured to be in her ninth decade. David tells me that this region consistently leans to the Left in politics and has an active organising committee who are responsible for such regular events as tonight's party.

'We're a few hours drive away from the Atlantic Coast or the Mediterranean, the ski-fields of the Pyrenees and an extra hour from Barcelona,' he says.

'You have found nirvana,' I admit.

David goes off to join Fred at the bar and toast their good fortune. I listen to the perfect Irish/English sung by a Frenchman and contemplate whether an Australian should attempt an Irish jig?

Accommodation: Douce France, Chemin d'Auvillar, Saint Nicolas de la Grave. Multi-lingual friendly hosts, swimming pool, wifi and excellent breakfast. Dinner on request. Double room E60, breakfast included. My score: 18/20.

Restaurant: A summer evening in the town square. Good food, Irish music and the whole town to dance with. My score: 17/20.

Distance cycled: 39 km

Actual distance: 39 km (the value of going in a circle!)

What I should have said: 'A Belgian, an Irishman, a Frenchman and an Australian walk into a bar...'

Chapter Six

cycling in the Tarn-Garonne

This morning, breakfast is a little later than usual due to the slow recovery from last night's festivities. Cathie is spending the day allowing her tired muscles to relax by the pool. I plead that Craig will get lazy if he's not worked every day. I can hear his cries of denial from the shed.

There's rain on the horizon as I set out. I hope it stays there. After a quick nod to the apple orchards, I pass a small landholding where a goat stands defiantly on the tin roof of a chicken coop. A chicken looks up at him as if to say, 'so what?' The goat bleats, a forlorn attempt at asserting his authority. The sheep in the same enclosure ignores him. The chicken goes back to digging in the dirt.

I turn onto a D road heading west between lush pastures where dairy cows are either eating hay or lying docilely in the grass. I wonder why they prefer hay to the grass? I cycle up a steep but short hill to the hamlet of Caumont which offers me a view of paddocks and orchards stretching all the way to the Garonne. There's only one shop open, a small epicure, but it's too early for lunch.

I join the D15 which slowly climbs a plateau one hundred and fifty metres above sea level where a blustery wind attempts to intimidate Craig and me. We fight back and amuse ourselves watching the curtain of rain approach from the horizon, wondering if it'll meet us before we reach shelter in the town of Lavit, eight kilometres away.

Short answer? Craig needed a wash anyway.

All that effort has made me hungry. Lavit, despite having a pharmacy and boucherie open on Sunday, has no restaurant. I'm baffled. It's a large town. I cycle the streets, turning down unlikely alleyways in the hope of success. Two boys follow me on their bikes, perhaps hoping I'll lead them to steak and frites? Non! The rain has stopped and a man vacuums his car at a newly installed car wash. I laugh at the incongruity of it all. A car wash but no restaurant.

Craig leads me down a minor road out of town which quickly makes me forget my hunger. The joys of the C road! We have a slight downhill and the wind is now behind us, so I let Craig have his way and he takes me through rows of hazelnut trees and apple orchards.

I love the serene beauty of the French farmhouse, built of stone with solid wooden shutters, occasionally featuring a decorative turret. In the garden are immaculate flowerbeds at the front, a timber or stone barn at one side and a vegetable garden on the other. Perhaps there'll be a disused pigeonnier or a greenhouse out the back. Usually there are ducks or chickens clucking around. There's always a stray cat somewhere on the edge of the scene, reclining in the sun. Of course there's a dog that barks and runs along the fence line whenever I pass, but never comes closer, even if the gate is open. All bark and no bite, thankfully.

Despite running roughly parallel to the road that brought me to Lavit, this lane has no traffic and I spend a cheerful hour with one hand on the handlebar, rarely pedalling and forgetting all about my empty stomach. I have nowhere to go and I'm going there at my own pace. I reflect on a book I read featuring the nearby town of Moissac, famous for its Saint Pierre Abbey, a stopover on the pilgrim route to Spain.

Hiding Edith is the story of a Jewish family escaping from the Nazis in the Second World War. Despite fleeing their native Austria into France, Edith's father is captured. Her mother takes Edith and her younger brother to Moissac where the children are cared for in a children's home. The courageous people of the town vowed to never reveal any details about the children in the institution. It's a beautiful story of kindness and hope in the face of terror.

Last night, David told me a much more recent story about Moissac which reminded me of *Hiding Edith*. In 2001, there was a huge chemical explosion in a factory in Toulouse which killed twenty-nine people and lead to thousands of injuries. So catastrophic was the disaster that thousands of people who lived near the factory had to be permanently relocated. Many of these citizens were North African immigrants from the poorer neighbourhoods. In a controversial move, the government decided to move these city-dwellers into the countryside with Moissac being the prime destination. I liked the symmetry of Moissac, once again, being a safe haven for those in need.

For Craig and I, it's downhill all the way to Castelmayan where the church has an impressive five bells but the bar and restaurant are both closed. In a park beside the river, one hundred people are having a barbecue lunch, the smell of fried meat drifts across the road to where I watch as the older men in the park leave their meals to begin a game of boules. I can barely stop myself from going over and pleading for any leftovers.

I finish the last of my water bottle and head back to Douce France. In the mid-afternoon, Cathie is swimming in the pool, Fred and David are drinking beer in the shade and I'm about to pounce on the remaining baguette left over from lunch. Craig smiles wanly. He considers this justice for dragging him out early on a Sunday.

Stale bread and hard cheese never tasted so good.

Accommodation: Douce France, Chemin d'Auvillar, Saint Nicolas de la Grave. Multi-lingual friendly hosts, swimming pool, wifi and excellent breakfast. Dinner on request. Double room E60, breakfast included. My score: 18/20.

Restaurant: Le Cadillac Restaurant, rue Gambetta, Saint Nicolas de la Grave. A popular haunt that specialises in large tasty pizzas and even larger meaty brochettes. Offers both indoor and outdoor tables and is worth a visit when Fred is having a night off. My score: 14/20

Distance cycled today: 41 km

Actual distance: 41 km (still going in a circle)

What I should have said: 'Dear Monsieur Boucher, would you be so kind as to cook me a faux filet, s'il vous plait?'

Chapter Seven

Saint Nicolas de la Grave to Toulouse

After another fine breakfast, we leave Fred and David at their farmhouse idyll and slowly cycle once more around Saint Nicolas. It really is a beautiful village with a particularly appealing war memorial alongside the church. Two pencil pines stand as guard of honour beside the plaque of a soldier and the list of names honouring the fallen warriors from the region. Christ watches from his Cross nearby.

It's a short downhill to rejoin the canal and the shade of the plane trees. A barge painted black and yellow waits on the left bank. On its deck are numerous pots of flowers and plants. A woman sits on a reclining chair at the bow, reading a book. It's the first of many barges we see that are now used as permanent homes, as though the Canal has become an outlying suburb of Toulouse.

At Montech we come across the curious *La Pente d'eau*, which loosely translates as *the water slope*, but is in fact, *a boat lift*. The lift consists of two train engines positioned either side of a sloping channel. The barge is seated between the two engines, fastened in an elaborate sash and slowly carried up the slope. The process takes twenty minutes and diverts the boat past five locks which would usually take up to an hour to navigate. It's ingenious... but currently out of service. A pity.

A man dressed in black walks on the canal path beside the boat lift. He wears a black cowboy hat and is carrying a fishing rod, slung casually over his shoulder. He whistles as he walks alongside the calm water. From his pocket he pulls a packet of cigarettes and casually lights one before sitting down under a tree and casting his line. I wonder if he's whistling a song about the trains that carry a boat up a slope?

Further on we come across an old moulin on the canal. A channel of water is diverted under the stone building to power the mill. Sadly, the windows are all boarded up and the signs painted on the side of the building hark from a different era. Opposite the moulin, a lock-keeper comes out from his house to begin the process of flooding the lock and preparing for the next vessel, a modern white barge flying a German flag. The Captain sits behind the wheel, shirtless, his skin pale in the brightening day. His wife prepares lunch on the deck. She waves a baguette as we cycle past. It makes me hungry.

At Grissolles, we stop under a rusting but still elegant wrought-iron covered market erected in 1894. There's only one restaurant in town and it's selling nothing but pizza. Not today, I'm afraid. We enter the lone boulangerie. The baker stands at the doorway smoking a cigarette as we order the last two sandwiches from his wife. Jambon and fromage it is.

On my last two trips to France, I've noticed a tendency on the part of boulangeries to offer sandwiches smeared with margarine instead of the customary butter. I find this rather sad, a sign that even the wonderful go-it-alone style of the French is being dictated to by the economic imperative. A Frenchman lives for his cheese, bread and butter. Margarine just doesn't cut it. I fear when they start cooking with oil not butter, all will be lost. We finish our sandwiches, wipe the stain of margarine from our lips and set off on the last stretch of Canal de Garonne into the rose-coloured city of Toulouse. But first, the outer suburbs.

For what seems like kilometres, the canal flows past a car marshalling yard. Thousands of shiny new vehicles are parked in ordered lots awaiting transportation. Our desire to own a new motor car every few years baffles me. I plan to keep Craig forever.

'Do you hear that, Craig?'

He dodges a tree root in answer and safely leads us over a steep bridge. How could I ever get rid of him after all we've been through? Thousands of kilometres up and down hills in Australia; across the breadth of France last year from the Atlantic Ocean to Germany. And two weeks ago when we were in the Italian Alps, Craig and I scaled the famous Passo Della Stelvio, a gut-busting climb over the second-highest mountain pass in the Alps. It took three hours and nearly killed us both but Craig never complained, even when the snowdrifts beside the road reached two metres. Admittedly he was a little shocked when a skier raced past a few metres away, but he kept his resolve and we made the summit only to find the other side blocked with snow. The road had only been open three days.

I lean down and pat his frame, 'You and me, Craig,' I say.

Cathie clears her throat.

'I was telling Craig he's more than a consumer item,' I say.

'I'm sure that made him very happy,' she replies, before stopping and consulting the map. With such a big city as Toulouse, the only adult on this journey has taken charge of directions.

Before finding our hotel we have to make a symbolic journey to Port de l'Embouchure where the Canal de Garonne, the Canal du Midi and the Canal de Brienne meet. It's a coffin-shaped port surrounded by city roads and honking traffic. A motorway looms to our right. In the middle of all this frantic modernity is a well-loved symbol of a slower age. A white marble bas-relief plaque of cherubs busy with shovels, no doubt building the canals, separates the Canal du Midi and the Canal de Brienne. The ever-present plane trees battle the pollution of a million cars and cast lovely shadows over the scene. Cathie and I take photos, naturally, for this is the end of our happy association with the Garonne and the beginning of our journey down the famed Canal du Midi.

But that journey begins tomorrow. Today, we find our hotel. Cathie has taken charge of directions. She leads me through numerous back roads, down busy streets of anxious delivery vans and shoppers carrying grocery bags, past hundreds of shops, alongside a railway line for a brief period, before one sharp right turn and here we are.

Cathie has booked this hotel, so not surprisingly, the man that greets us at reception is very handsome with swept-back hair, an open-necked shirt, tight trousers and suede loafers. He smiles a little too much at my wife but generously offers us a secure courtyard to leave Craig and Jenny. He shows us to our rather basic room which is on the ground-floor and has double-glazed windows and metal shutters.

Dear Reader, there is a ritual I feel I must inform you of. I'll only do it once, but make no mistake, it happens every day on every bicycle journey. The washing of lycra in the hand-basin. If you feel squeamish, please skip the next paragraph.

Both of us strip naked and toss our clothes into the soapy water. Cathie has the good sense to shower while the clothes are soaking. I sit on our bed and check emails and take notes. Yes, still naked. After a few minutes I attempt a cursory churning motion in the hand-basin, squeezing our shorts and jerseys once before refilling the basin with clean water. Cathie gets dressed while I jump in the shower. Cathie then does a much more efficient job of rinsing the clothes, rolling each item in a hand towel and squeezing tightly before draping the garments on clothes hangers. With two pairs of shorts and shirts each, we have one days grace for drying.

What took me one hundred words and a few minutes to describe is the hardest job of the day, particularly after an eighty kilometre cycle. I promise no more talk of such matters.

Laundry finished and wearing suitable daytime clothes, we explore the beautiful city of Toulouse. It starts to rain as we reach the lovely Capitole square in the city. The umbrellas are up at every outdoor cafe and most diners and drinkers seem unperturbed by the change in the weather. We wander the streets with mouths agape at the simple beauty of many of the buildings, their delicate pink-rose colour seems to soak in the light. They are luminous in the late afternoon. At times and from certain angles, they remind me of Australia's Uluru - the giant rock in the centre of the outback.

Visitors travel thousands of miles to see the changing hues of the rock face as the sun sets. From delicate pink through to ochre and dark purple by sunset, Uluru is one of the natural wonders of the world. The buildings of Toulouse while not quite so extravagant in colour have that same timelessness and aura about them.

We wander the city streets until evening when we happen upon a vegetarian restaurant in a quiet back alley that offers four courses for thirteen Euros. It's a tight little room with serving areas around the outside. The deal is simple, you help yourself to as much as you want from each course.

So ends the myth that the French are light eaters. Over the next two hours, I enjoy watching slim young French women devour huge plates stacked with quiche, salad, rice and vegetable-bourgignon before moving onto the dessert tray with gusto. The couple beside us, a wavy-haired young woman and her hipster boyfriend, eat a total of eleven slices of quiche between them. Yes, I counted. Cathie and I, gluttons that we are, managed only six although I will admit to three trips to the dessert station. Fromage blanc, custard and apple crumble and fruit salad to fool myself I was eating healthy. I normally steer away from all-you-can-eat restaurants, finding the quality always below standard. But in defence of the young couple beside us, the quiche is fantastic. I'm tempted to have a post-dessert slice but choose another glass of sauvignon blanc instead. Cathie and I reason we're stocking up for the hard kilometres ahead on the Canal du Midi.

We make our way back to the hotel and the suave man at reception asks us when we want breakfast. I'm tempted to say December, but suggest seven o'clock instead. He nods at me and smiles at Cathie.

Accommodation: Hotel Alize, 17 rue Baque, Toulouse. Cheap simple rooms close to the city centre and the canal. Space for bikes, wifi, good breakfast and helpful (handsome) staff. Double E55. My score: 14/20.

Restaurant: La Faim des Haricots, 3 rue du Puits Vert, Toulouse. Don't eat for hours before arriving at this friendly engaging vegetarian restaurant. The staff are smiling and helpful, the food is plentiful and it's a welcome relief from the heavy sauces and meat of typical French dining. Excellent value. My score: 16/20.

Distance cycled: 76 km

Actual distance: 71 km

What I should have said: 'Pardon Monsieur, she is my wife, not my sister.'

Chapter Eight

Toulouse to Castelnaudary

The Canal du Midi is one of the engineering wonders of the world. Work commenced on building the canal in April 1667, the brainchild of merchant Pierre Paul Riquet who dreamed of a safe shipping route from Bordeaux to the Mediterranean. This would allow boats to avoid the treacherous circumnavigation of the Iberian Peninsula, saving time and money and avoiding the hazards of storms and Barbary pirates.

For two centuries, the Canal fulfilled Riquet's vision until the arrival of the railways which provided a cheaper and faster cargo option in the late 19th century. Even so, it's interesting to note that the last commercial barges travelled the Canal as recently as 1970. The only cargo meandering along the 240-kilometre waterway now are tourists, content to putter along at a stately eight kilometres per hour.

The Canal du Midi holds a certain mystique among travellers. If you ask many people what their dream holiday in France would be, they'll state the obvious such as a week in a Paris apartment followed by a meander through the vineyards of Provence and perhaps a ski adventure in the Alps. But not far behind this dream list is always a longing to float down the Canal du Midi. The canal has an almost mythical other-worldly romance to it. Before coming here, I'd tell people we were going to cycle the towpath and they'd get a distant look in their eyes and mention regal barges, ancient locks and picnics under the plane trees.

But for Cathie and I, eight kilometres per hour, reclining on a deckchair listening to the rhythmic putter of the ship's motor for day upon day is a dream too far. We prefer Craig and Jenny and the chance to wander off into canal-side villages and up into the hills surrounding the waterway.

The Canal du Midi flows from Toulouse to Sete through some of France's most beautiful and alluring countryside: rolling plains of wheat and sunflowers, vineyards, dry mountain ranges, swampland and coastal marshes. It's a cycling trip through the rural essence of France where the slow pace of village life matches the flow of water between the bustling city of Toulouse and the resort town of Sete on the Mediterranean.

It's also a procession through a bloodstained land of ancient persecution and religious crusades where the local Cathar population were mercilessly slaughtered at the behest of the Catholic Church during the Albigensian Crusades of the 13th and 14th Century.

****

The handsome man at hotel reception provides an excellent breakfast this morning. If I'm not mistaken, his shirt is unbuttoned even more today and he smiles at Cathie so much while pouring her coffee I fear her cup will overflow. He offers me a cursory refill. But he is enough of a gallant to help us both remove Craig and Jenny from their overnight nook.

With unerring accuracy, Cathie finds the canal pathway after a few minutes of peak-hour manoeuvring. I breathe a sigh of relief to be off the roads. Now we only have to dodge the homeless. The downtrodden and less-fortunate citizens of Toulouse have made a home with cast-off mattresses and blankets under the shelter of the road bridges spanning the canal. We decide to keep to the upper cycle path, joining the hundreds of commuter cyclists racing to work. Craig and Jenny are buffeted to the far right of the path as office workers and students rush to meet a deadline.

However, I will admit to the smirking joy I always feel when stopped at a traffic light beside a long line of cars carrying commuters. It's not a nice character trait, but I can't help but feel privileged to be cycling for a day rather than heading to an office and a soulless computer screen.

After six kilometres, we're finally free of the traffic noise and cycle anarchy. The canal is shaded by plane trees and the western sky has the complexion of oncoming showers. We pass three blocks of high-rise apartments and the saddest sports field I've ever seen. Football and Rugby goalposts stand lonely at an awkward angle in two-metre high grass, surrounded by a car park. I look up at the apartment blocks and wonder where the children who live there play? Further on, a rusted Peugeot is on blocks, the front door open, the windscreen smashed. Along the canal are lines of barges, some look disused and abandoned, some are beautifully renovated with sparkling paint jobs, new curtains and flowerpots on deck. There's a barge repair marina on the left bank which appears to be doing a roaring trade restoring the old workhorses. Who doesn't dream of living on a barge?

Craig is not changing gear as he should, allowing me only four gears out of a possible seven on the rear cog. I stop to fiddle. Cathie waits patiently beside me. A woman jogger runs on the spot and asks if we'd like her to take our photo. She has wispy blond hair and is wearing lemon running pants and a cream top. Her shoes appear to be brand-new. Perhaps she's just looking to have a rest? I'd like to oblige and pose but Craig needs attention. The woman waves goodbye and sets off at a brisk jog, her new shoes effortlessly dodging the mud puddles.

Despite my best efforts, Craig continues to allow only limited gearing so we struggle along together, both silently cursing the other. I'm tempted to say Craig's having a tantrum of neglect but I fear he'll only get worse.

We settle into a rhythm, Cathie and Jenny breeze along in front while Craig and I clank behind. I'm pleased to be free of the noise and clutter of Toulouse and back among the plane trees where the artistry of sunshine works its magic. The weather is improving and the dappled light and elegant shadows under the canopy of green is a marvel. Too frequently for Craig, I stop and take a photo of the canal ahead, the perfect frame of trees and lush greenery as the channel gently meanders off stage. It's the image of a thousand guidebooks - majestic, serene and inviting. It only needs a cyclist or a barge to complete the image. Cathie and Jenny oblige.

At Montgiscard, we stop to admire the lock and an ancient lavoir on the opposite bank. Behind the lavoir is a cafe but the only way to get there is to cross the lock gates. A sign forbids this. We look both ways and like errant children, scurry across.

We are punished for our misdemeanour by enduring the barista from hell. He's a middle-aged man with pleated grey trousers pulled up way too high, a pale blue shirt and a distinctive combover. I order two cafe au lait. He fills the group head of the espresso machine and places two cups underneath. He then presses the button and allows the coffee to espress into each cup for much too long. Tepid brown water dribbles into our cup. He then adds a pinch of cold milk to each cup and individually froths the contents of the cup under the spout. I kid you not. We both wince at the sound as he boils the life out of it.

We take the poison outside and sit in the weak sunshine. It tastes burnt and bitter, even after the addition of two sugars. We sigh. It's a lovely vista though - the lavoir, a barge rising gently to the correct level in the lock, a hawk hovering over a vineyard, two cyclists pretending to enjoy a refreshing coffee. I vow never to cross the lock gates again... after we return to our bikes.

The stone bridges spanning the canal hark back to the colours of Toulouse. Built of narrow brick, they are simple and elegant structures that we never miss the opportunity to cycle across. They change colour according to the time of day, from pink rose in the morning to dark burgundy in the evening.

Villefranche-de-Lauragais is a bastide town that owes its existence to the pastel trade of the 17th century. Built on the Via Aquitania, an ancient Roman road, it has a number of elegant faded shopfronts and a church with a distinctive tower of six bells, which are ringing right now signalling lunchtime for weary cyclists. We choose a restaurant with tables scattered around a tree-lined square. The owner is a burly gruff man who looks like he knows his way around a rugby field. I hope his wife is doing the cooking. The three-course meal costs the princely sum of twelve Euros and consists of a salad for starter, a cassoulet for main and the usual suspects for dessert. The guilty choose crème brûlée. It's hardly inspiring fare, but it's pleasant to sit under the oak trees, drink rosé and contemplate how far we have to cycle in the afternoon. When I enter the bar to pay the bill, I notice the rugby scarves of the local Toulouse club strung behind the counter.

Back to the canal. Our next stop is the curious Port Lauragais which I can only describe as a truck-stop for canal users. There's a wide expansive port for mooring, a tourist office, a restaurant, a bar, a hotel and a car park. But there is no village. It's solely for people to moor their boats and use the amenities.

A toilet stop.

We ride around the car park, consider visiting the tourist shop, contemplate a gelato at the bar and wonder how much a room at the hotel costs before deciding we'd prefer our services provided by a 17th century village, not a lonely circle of modern buildings.

I can't possibly ride past the obelisk dedicated to the visionary Riquet without detouring to pay my respects. We slosh along a tree-lined muddy path following signs to the monument. When we stop near an old moulin, two women approach. The younger one, with an Irish accent, asks me if this is the way to Carcassonne? She points down a lonely road. I shake my head and direct her towards the canal. It's mid-afternoon and they have another sixty kilometres of bumpy path before they reach the Cite Medieval. They'll need the luck of the Irish.

Pierre Paul Riquet deserves better than a grey monument on a hill surrounded by an imposing wall and a padlocked gate. The grass in the enclosure is overgrown and the whole area has an air of forlorn neglect. Even the birds sound muted. We are the only visitors.

The first shop I notice when cycling up the main street of Castelnaudary in the late afternoon is a magasin du velo. The owner is a hunched old man who lovingly puts Craig on a bike lift and fiddles with his gears. It takes him a few seconds to notice what I ignored all day. Craig has a frayed gear cable that needs replacing. The owner promises to do it within the hour. Cathie and I carry our panniers two hundred metres up the road to our hotel situated near the main square.

We wash quickly and celebrate our arrival at the cassoulet capital of the world with a beer at the bar. An hour later, Craig is fitted with a new cable and he positively speeds up the hill to his room for the night.

I have eaten cassoulet a number of times but always found it to be claggy and heavy. The beans are mush, the sausage tasteless and the duck fatty and overcooked. But tonight, in the home of the famous dish, I hope for better. Cathie and I walk the streets looking at the menu and decor of each restaurant, trying to decide who will offer the premier meal. Finally, down a narrow street we come upon the La Belle Epoque. A sign above the door announces that the chef is a member of the Master Cassoulet Fraternity of Castelnaudary. I have no idea what this means but it's as good a recommendation as any.

We take an outside table and a woman informs us that we are too early for dinner but she'll be happy to take our drinks order. No worries. When my cassoulet finally arrives, it's superb. The beans are cooked to perfection, the duck fleshy and tasty, the sausage spicy. I devour the contents of the earthenware bowl and use the last remaining bread to mop up the juices. At last I can understand what all the hype is about. I'm a sucker for stews and casseroles and this peasant dish is among my favourites. How can you go wrong with haricot beans, duck and pork sausage? I forgive the waiter her haughtiness. It must be tough to be married to an artisan chef who cooks meals that will stick to your insides for days afterwards.

We slowly walk back to our hotel only to discover a cycle criterium is taking place outside our front door. Thirty fit young men are racing gleaming road bikes up our street, turning sharp left at the town square and hurtling down the parallel street before turning at the bottom and repeating the circuit time and time again. I glance at my watch. It's nine in the evening. We take a seat in a bar trackside and watch the spectacle. It goes on and on. At 10:30, I'm tired from cassoulet, alcohol and watching these cyclist push themselves to the point of exhaustion. I decide it's a sport for the young. We retire to our room. I can hear the hum of narrow tyres on bitumen as I fall asleep.

Accommodation: Hotel Du Centre Et Du Lauragais, 31 Cours De La Republique. Good breakfast, wifi, comfortable rooms, excellent location in the centre of town, quality restaurant, if perhaps a little expensive. Double room E50, breakfast extra. My score: 15/20

Restaurant: La Belle Epoque, 55 rue General Dejean. Tasty authentic cassoulet, pleasant atmosphere, good value. My score: 15/20.

In my hotel, I read about the origins of Cassoulet. Apparently, Castelnaudary was under siege from the English at one point in the Hundred Years War and supplies were running low. The women collected all the remaining food and cooked a nourishing meal for the town's defenders. After eating this meal, consisting of meat, beans and a few vegetables, legend has it that the French soldiers attacked the English with such ferocity that the siege was broken and the town saved. Such is the power of cassoulet... and a good story. The dish is named after the earthenware pot it's cooked in.

Distance cycled: 76 km
Actual distance: 64 km

What I should have said: 'Monsieur, you make coffee like I speak French!'

Chapter Nine

Castelnaudary to Carcassonne

I poke my head out of the hotel window this morning half-expecting to see the cyclists still surging through their laps but the streets are deserted.

Breakfast is a treat in a grand dining room with linen napkins and polished cutlery. Pity we arrive dressed in lycra and dusty shoes.

I always judge a French breakfast in two ways. Firstly, the quality of the croissants. The flaky offerings this morning are freshly made, not frozen and reheated. The more flakes I have on my plate to clean up, the better the croissant. Secondly, if the hotel offers yoghurt in glass jars accompanied by fresh fruit, then I'm in ecstasy. The Hotel du Centre excels in both categories.

Suitably fed, we carry our panniers across the street to where Craig and Jenny have been staying in the basement room of a bar. I open the door... and the room is empty.

'Craig has been kidnapped!' I call.

Cathie comes down the stairs, looks into the empty room and points to the door in the far corner.

'Where's that lead?' she asks.

I rush across, fling open the door and find Jenny and Craig leaning at an odd angle against the cool room door. I touch Craig's handlebars. He's cold.

'Found them,' I call.

'Well done,' Cathie says, irony heavy in her tone.

We carry them upstairs to the warming sunshine. Despite Craig having a new gear cable, he sounds unhappy as we set out. In fact, as we near the expansive Castelnaudary port, he throws his chain. Cathie admires the view while I coax Craig back into working order.

A swan glides around an island in the port, twenty sleek boats wait for hire and Craig is finally willing to co-operate. I wash my greasy hands in the canal water and wipe them on the grass. The seven hectares of open water in the port shimmers in the early morning light. On the left bank, the houses are elegant silhouettes with the sun rising behind. Castelnaudary was the first stop from Toulouse for travellers on the passenger barges of times past.

This morning, we cycle carefully between tourists loading oversized suitcases onto the rental barges. How many clothes do you need for a week on a barge? Surely all that's required is a pair of shorts, a shirt, a carton of beer and a vast array of reading material to pass the slow hours? Incredibly, people are carrying tennis racquets, skates, a football and fishing rods onto the sleek deck of a Crown Blue Line vessel. I'm tempted to suggest they toss everything overboard and replace it with two bicycles, but who am I to judge how people spend their holiday.

'Right, Craig?'

No answer. It wasn't me who put him in the cool room!

A few kilometres out of Castelnaudary the path becomes bumpy and overgrown with grass. It's little more than a walking track with exposed tree roots, mud patches and wheel ruts. We spend the next thirty minutes dodging the obstacles rather than looking at the serene tree-lined canal. We experienced a similar episode yesterday. For a path that is justly world famous for cycling, I didn't expect it to be in such poor condition. In certain sections I wouldn't even describe it as a path. It appears as if no government authority does routine maintenance. No-one is responsible for the upkeep, except cyclists and walkers who trudge out a path through the undergrowth and between the puddles and tree roots.

During my cycle across France last year, the paths of the Loire and Soane Rivers were kept in good condition being either bitumen or firm well-maintained gravel. There were regular signs directing the traveller to nearby villages. Astonishingly, even the Canal de Garonne is in much better repair than its more famous sister.

A pity.

Despite this, the canal is beautiful this morning with leaves floating on the still water. It's as though we're cycling through a cathedral of trees, so awe-inspiring is the ceiling of green. I can think of no better place to worship.

Near Bram, we turn off the path and follow the signs into the village beside fields of garlic and lettuce. There are two boulangeries in town and we choose the one with the longest line of customers. The plump lady behind the counter sells us two soft oozy almond croissants that we devour in a park, accompanied by suitably expressive 'oohs' and 'ahhs.'

Bram has circular streets in a fortified arrangement but the only invaders now are cyclists and walkers seeking pastries.

We sit on the rear pew of a dark quiet church which has six large candles above the altar.

'Do they burn them each Sunday?' I whisper.

'Or only for special occasions?' Cathie suggests.

When I was a teenager, I used to hitchhike around Australia and whenever I was stranded in a town with little money and nowhere to sleep, I'd always choose a Catholic church to enter late in the evening. The door was unlocked and I'd fall asleep on a pew or on the carpeted floor, with the statue of Jesus looking down on me. I've enjoyed the quiet calm of church interiors ever since.

The history of Bram is blood-soaked. In the 13th century, this was a Cathar stronghold until the murderous Simon de Monfort leading the Catholic forces captured the town after three bloody days of fighting. The crazy victor ordered that all male survivors have their eyes gouged out as an example to others not to defy the Catholic rule. One man was spared this macabre punishment and assigned the job of leading the disfigured survivors to safety.

It's a horrible story, more so given the Cathar religion reads as a simple and dare I say it, sensible doctrine. The followers believed in not eating meat, not swearing oaths or telling lies, equality between the sexes and living a spiritual existence free of the trappings of wealth.

In the 12th Century, this appealing doctrine took root in the region and by its very existence threatened the Catholic Church. The Pope, with the unearned title of Innocent the Third, called for a Crusade against the Cathars, appointing a series of military leaders to his Holy Army. An estimated five hundred thousand believers were murdered in the Crusade because the Catholic Church ruthlessly understood that power was all that mattered.

Back on the canal path, we pass a boat flying an Australian flag. We wave and call, 'g'day.' The man relaxing on a deckchair holds up a beer in answer. We arrive at a bridge where two cyclists without panniers are trying to decide which path to take. We stop beside them. The choices are a bitumen road on the right bank, or a bumpy narrow path on the left.

I smile at the cyclists.

'If it's bumpy, it's the canal path,' I say, and set off. Cathie follows.

At the next bend I look back and see that the two cyclists aren't behind us. I look across to the right bank. The woman leads, the man follows with his hands clasped behind his head, enjoying the smooth surface.

'The road will turn off soon and they'll be stranded,' I say.

I dodge a tree root and slosh through a puddle, splattering mud on my legs. We lose sight of the young cyclists.

Two kilometres further along, when we arrive at Beteille lock, the very same cyclists are stretched out on the lush green grass. The man has his arm around the girl's waist, her head rests on his chest. They look very relaxed.

Cathie clears her throat. She doesn't have to say a word.

After three hours of bumping and weaving at a snail's pace, we decide to detour through the town of Pezens, hoping to find a restaurant. It's a glorious C road winding over a hill shaded by trees and through a series of vineyards. We cycle along at a leisurely sixteen kilometres per hour, marvelling at the smoothness of the road. We don't mind that Pezens doesn't have an open restaurant. At least there's a boulangerie. We wait to be served as the lady behind the counter helps two elderly customers load twenty large cakes into a Citroen van. That's two hundred Euros of confectionery. I'd like to be going to that party. We make do with two baguettes of jambon and fromage and yes... margarine. C'est la vie.

I consult the map.

'We can go back to the canal,' I say, 'or follow this road all the way into Carcassonne.'

'How far on the road?' Cathie asks.

'Maybe five kilometres,' I guess, 'but it may be quite busy.'

'Better busy than bumpy,' she answers.

We cycle up a steep hill and at the crest have a lovely view over vineyards to the Cite Medieval, with the lower town spreading out from its base. Every time I see Carcassonne, I'm captivated by the fairytale vision of a fortress on a hill with all those peaked turrets. I half-expect a posse of Knights to gallop across the moat, swords drawn, flags fluttering, Sean Connery at the front.

We cruise downhill into the madness of strip shopping in the new town. We cycle on footpaths to avoid the traffic and eventually cross the canal. I look down. There is no canal path whatsoever, not even a walking track. I'm pleased we took the detour.

We arrive at our Bed and Breakfast to read a note on the front gate. No-one here until five pm. It's three o'clock.

'How about a coffee and ice cream,' Cathie suggests.

We roll into the main square of the lower town and choose the busiest cafe.

Many years ago, when I was young and had hair and wore tight clothes and pretended I was hip, I travelled around France with a newly married couple and their angelic nine-month-old baby daughter. It was very generous of them to tolerate a would-be hipster who demanded the front seat because he got car sick. Each afternoon we would arrive at a different town and they would spend an hour ferrying me to a variety of the worst hotels available until I finally settled on the cheapest. They'd leave me there and drive off to their much more expensive and comfortable hotel, with plans to meet up for dinner.

By day, they liked visiting chateaus. I objected to paying the exorbitant entry fees and would usually wander the nearest village streets until they'd completed their opulent tour. In Carcassonne, I flatly refused to even venture up to the Cite Medieval, so certain was I that it wasn't worth the money. I walked a derelict area of the new town, eating a reheated croque monsieur for lunch and cursing my lack of money. While my friends wandered the enchanted streets of a hilltop fortress, I sat in a park and counted ducks. When we met later, they laughed and told me there was no entry fee. It was a town, not a chateau. I'd missed my chance. We still joke about it thirty years on.

We check into our B&B and the kindly owner gives us a front room on the top floor. I open the window and there on the hill is the Cite.

'Free entry,' I say to myself.

In the evening, we walk from our B&B across the elegant Pont Vieux and up the hill to the fortress. Cathie and I visited Carcassonne in 2010 and we're hoping to find the same restaurant. It shouldn't be difficult. How many restaurants are there in a tourist mecca? It only takes an hour to locate the Restaurant La Plo. But it's worth it.

The Cite has been occupied since Roman times with each invading army adding to its splendour. There are many conflicting views on how it was named, but my favourite is that it derives from Carcas, the widow of a Muslim prince who captured the fort in the

8th century. When the Prince died in battle, his wife donned his garments and lead the army against Emperor Charlemagne. The Cite was under siege and all appeared lost when Carcas ordered that the last remaining pig be fed grain and hurled over the wall at the opposing troops. On seeing this flagrant waste of food, Charlemagne was convinced that the fortress was well-provisioned and unlikely to be successfully stormed. He lifted the siege and the church bells rang in the Cite, giving rise to the call 'Carcas sonne.'

If nothing else, I'd bet on Carcas over Charlemagne in a card game. She'd beat him with a pair of eights.

After falling into decline in the 17th century, a local mayor, Jean-Pierre Cros-Mayrevieille, convinced the French government to fund restoration which began in the 1840s. Although criticised by many during its restoration, the architect Eugene Viollet-le-Duc created a masterpiece of double remparts and fifty-three towers. A florid whimsy or a magical fortress? It hardly matters to the tourists who arrive in increasing numbers every year.

Accommodation: Au Domisiladore B&B, 19 boulevard Marcou, Carcassonne. Friendly host, large rooms, wifi, good breakfast, located in the lower town and a twenty-minute walk from the Cite. Double E57, including breakfast. My score: 15/20

Restaurant: Restaurant le Plo, 23 rue du Plo, Carcassonne Cite Medieval. Among the numerous restaurants in the Cite, le Plo stands out as being good value and having a pleasant atmosphere. We chose the three-course formule menu for E19. The entree was an excellent cherve chaud salad, with the cheese being wrapped in 'money bag' pastry. The main course was duck breast with a fig sauce, accompanied by delicious disc-shaped chips (I remembered them from three years ago!). We had the obligatory crème brûlée for dessert. The waitress, with tattoos on her arms, was friendly and efficient and enjoyed her work so much she danced behind the bar for her own amusement when not ferrying plates to we diners.

Splendid! My score: 16/20

Distance cycled: 47 km

Actual distance: 39 km

What I should have said: 'Me, lost? Mon dieu, non!'

Chapter Ten

Carcassonne to Bize-Minervois

Monsieur serves us an early breakfast in his back yard greenhouse. He's a gentle, kind man with a dry sense of humour and much better English than he likes to admit. He offers us the local French newspaper to 'enjoy with your croissant.' I could always look at the photos, I suppose?

The streets are very quiet this morning, a lone street-sweeping machine driven by a man with a red beanie is the only activity. We cross the bridge at the port and trundle along the left bank of the channel. I look to the right and glimpse the fairytale Cite Medieval one last time. It's a rare opportunity to see two UNESCO World Heritage sites at the same time - the Canal and the Cite.

We cycle under a road bridge. The pavement is strewn with broken glass but we hopefully dodge the worst. After crossing the impressive Pont Canal du Fresquel, we gingerly ride across the appropriately named *gue* - a spillover that is slippery and green with slime. I grip the handlebars just that little bit tighter.

'Gue phew,' I say.

The canal winds merrily along, more like a river than a man-made channel. The value of a bend in the canal is the sense of anticipation. My gaze is constantly drawn forward, admiring the beauty of the plane trees but also sensing the changing scenery. The bend represents the enclosed human-scaled vista as opposed to the endless expanse of the straight Canal de Garonne.

The Canal du Midi is a tiny landscape, accessible and attainable. It's designed for enjoyment at eight kilometres per hour. Another barge approaches us from the bend. Yet another Australian flag flutters from the rear. Perhaps that's why so many Australians are attracted to the Canal. We come from a land that is overpowering in its featurelessness, a land of sweeping plains and wide horizons. The

Canal is like a child's toy landscape in comparison and much more attractive for being that way.

As we approach Eveque lock, Cathie says those few words I've been dreading.

'My tyre feels flat.'

Sure enough, her front tyre has a puncture, no doubt the result of the glass back at Carcassonne. It must be a very slow leak. We park under the shade of a tree beside the lock-keepers house and I set about repairing it. I decide that even though we have a spare tube, I'll patch the existing one as soon as I find the pinprick hole. This requires me pumping up the tube and running down to the lock, leaning over and submerging it in water. Yep, the bubbles are... just there. Back to the repair kit and after only twenty minutes and some mild cursing, the tyre is back on the wheel and Cathie is away.

She goes no further than two metres when I notice her rear tyre is also flat. Merde! I knew we wouldn't escape that glass under the bridge so easily.

Another thirty minutes with an extra quick trip to the lock water in search of bubbles, this time watched by an amused lock-keeper. We set off again, having lost the better part of an hour. The sun is high in the sky and the temperature rising noticeably.

We are now in the Mediterranean south where the climate is drier and hotter than the more humid Atlantic stretch of the canal. The houses are more likely to be built of stone not brick and topped with Spanish-style roof tiles.

At Trebes, we stop at the only boulangerie and buy mini-escargots and local biscuits, sweet and baked with almond meal. We sit at the port and eat them all. I keep glancing at Jenny's tyres. So far so good. Craig has a superior air about him this morning that is most unbecoming. It's a very busy port with boats lined up along the dock, waiters ferrying coffee and cake to diners sitting beside the water, cyclists stocking up on supplies for picnics and amongst it all, a dog sleeping under a table.

It's hot and windy, blowing straight into our faces as we leave Trebes. The path is skittish gravel. On one slight descent, four young people pass riding heavily-laden road bikes with thin tyres. One of the girls applies her brakes too sharply at the bottom of the hill and skids in the gravel, toppling off onto the grass. We help her to her feet. She's not hurt, luckily, but with such thin tyres... on this path. It will be difficult. With the abandon of youth, they quickly ride away.

The path leads through a narrow cutting with a high red cliff wall on the left bank. I'm admiring the colour when a snake slithers across the way immediately ahead. I instinctively raise my feet from the pedals and call out to warn Cathie. One of us also issues a very girly shriek, but I won't embarrass him by saying who it is. I hate snakes! I'm sure this fellow isn't poisonous, but it does little to calm my nerves.

I remember riding my mountain bike through the National Park in the Blue Mountains where we live. Inevitably, in summer, I'd be barrelling down a steep dusty incline only to see a brown snake slithering across the path ahead. Australia has eleven of the twelve deadliest snakes on the planet. We also have copperheads, deadly but more docile than the brown snake, in our backyard. I usually come across a serpent sunning himself in the grass, once a year. We both turn and flee. Only one of us is shrieking.

Two flat tyres and a snake. What else can happen today?

Lunch, hopefully.

But first we enjoy the madcap humour and creativity of Joel Barthes, the lock-keeper at Aiguille lock. No doubt bored with hours spent waiting for the next barge, Monsieur Barthes has created a wonderland of wood carvings and metal sculptures that line the right bank.

There's a crocodile ready to jump aboard the barge as it leaves the lock; a trio of clucking hens look on in amusement; a French poodle prances; a snake charmer plays his flute in front of the rearing serpent; a spider made from a gas tank wiggles beside a metal family of wacky proportions.

The piece de resistance is a compound of moving sculptures that spring into life every few minutes - a lady cycles on a bike, a man playfully slaps another man, a six-armed green object dances. Monsieur Barthes is a master craftsman in iron and wood and his canal-side exhibition should be world-famous.

We're out of drinking water and hot and hungry when we detour to Puicheric. There's only one restaurant open. The owner greets us at the door. There are no other diners. I suggest we eat outside in the shade of the balcony. He shakes his head, instead ushering us into the humid main dining room. He offers us the lunch menu. There appears to be no formule menu today. I ask why? He shrugs. Only expensive main courses. This does not look promising. Unimpressed with his off-hand manner, we decide to leave. It can't be too far to the next village. He shrugs again, indifferent.

Despite the well-worn cliche of all French waiters being aloof and disinterested, it has not been my experience. We've always found the French to be patient, humourous and helpful. Except this chap in Puicheric.

La Redorte is a lovely village with a very crowded port side restaurant. We hurry across the bridge and park Craig and Jenny in the shade. Most of the diners are finishing their meals, a few already indulging in dessert. There's only one vacant table... next to a large group who've finished their steak and frites and are now all lighting the obligatory post-lunch cigarette. Oh dear.

It can't be far to the next village...

We cross the eleven-arched Ourages de l'Argentdouble, surely one of the wonders of the Canal. Built in 1693, it's an elegant spillover from the canal into the Argentdouble river below. We cycle across the cobblestones slowly, in due reverence.

At Jouarres lock, we buy a can of Coke and pretend it's our lunch.

It's 2:30 in the afternoon when we arrive at Homps and spy a small snack bar on the left bank. It has a few outdoor tables where people are eating pizza. We walk under the cool balcony and take a seat. The owner, a tall man with wavy hair and a large moustache grimaces when we order a pizza to share. He looks imploringly to his wife, the chef. It appears she has stopped cooking for the day. Perhaps they notice the slump of my shoulders, or maybe they're like most French people - helpful and kind. Whatever the answer, soon we are tucking into a tasty jambon pizza with just the right proportion of sauce and fromage, washed down with a spritely pichet de rosé. Merci, merci, merci.

After eating, Cathie walks to the fountain along the bank to fill our water bottle... and almost steps on another serpent! At the start of summer, the snakes are enjoying the sunshine.

We leave the canal at Homps and cycle along a D-road, heading to our Bed and Breakfast for the evening, somewhere in the Minervois foothills. We're pushed along the road by a stiff tailwind and the speeding traffic. Scotch bloom competes with grapevines in the dry fields and we lose count of the number of dead snakes on the road.

Bize-Minervois is a beau-village with a lovely river, narrow cool alleyways, a regal bridge and an archway announcing our arrival. The owners of the B&B are a British couple, the taciturn Dennis from Scotland and the lovely Hilary from Yorkshire. They are the perfect hosts. First thing Dennis offers is a beer in the garden, followed by a swim in their pool. Lovely. We are already so enchanted with the property we ask if they have a vacancy for tomorrow night as well. They do. I drink another beer and forget all about flat tyres, snakes and dusty paths.

Accommodation: Maison des Palmiers, 12 Avenue de l'Amiral Narbonne, Bize-Minervois. Lovely hosts, wonderful breakfast, wifi, pool, outdoor dining, garage for bikes, peaceful village. Double E55-75, depending on choice of rooms, breakfast included. My score: 18/20.

Restaurant: Cafe Canal du Midi, 1 Place le Herbes, Bize-Minervois. We walk through the arched entry to the village and come upon this excellent restaurant. For dinner, we have a table near the window and choose the three-course formule menu. Entree is a delicious and original version of the ubiquitous chevre chaud salad. It's a Paris-Brest pastry inspired ring of choux pastry with cherve cheese and duck ham, sprinkled with balsamic vinegar and circled by an accompanying salad. A surprising lovely textured dish. Main course is steak and frites cooked to perfection. Dessert is a jar of home-made jelly and fruit salad which tastes much better than it reads. It's a warm welcoming space with a enchanting view through the archway. The cost for the formule menu is E19. Highly recommended. My score: 18/20

Distance cycled: 59 km

Actual distance: 51 km

What I should have said: 'Monsieur, avez vous serpent on the menu, s'il vous plait?'

Chapter Eleven

A cycle through the Minervois region

Dennis and Hilary are both trained in customer service, with Dennis spending many years in the hotel industry and Hilary running a popular cafe for two decades. We are in good hands. Breakfast is a treat in the garden under the umbrellas. We meet the other guests, two elderly Scottish couples who share Dennis's dry humour. We talk golf, football and midges - their absence on the Canal and their abundance on the Scottish coast. Dennis tells us he's planning a dinner tonight. At nineteen Euros with all the wine we can drink and Dennis's talent in the kitchen, how can we refuse?

Today's ride has the historic village of Minervre as the destination. On a sunny but cool morning, we cycle across the old bridge over the La Cesse river and head slowly uphill beside the stream, with vineyards and stony hills to our right. Everywhere there is scotch bloom and I make a mental note to ask Dennis what the Scots call this troublesome weed. As is usual in France, the grape vines are growing in brittle rocky ground. I salute the genius of a culture that can get such abundance from so little.

Hilary has suggested this quiet back road and I can immediately see why. The only car we've seen in thirty minutes has been a farmer's white Renault van. He parks up ahead and inspects his vines. He waves as we pass. The roads closely follows the river and we can see the clear water tumbling over pale rocks. In the sleepy village of Agel, we drink from a tap supplied by a spring somewhere in the mountains above. A few workmen dismantle a tent on the grounds of the chateau. There was wedding here yesterday. Two men wheel bicycles along the footpath, the older one wears a beret and gestures with one hand as he talks. They lean their bikes against the chateau wall and sit on the bench seat to continue their conversation. The older one now gestures with both hands. I imagine he's talking about the wedding. Agel has a lovely open bell tower with two bells and streets of old stone houses.

We cycle on, still steadily climbing, to the more modern village of Aigues-Vives where we sit in the square and share the chocolate croissant saved from breakfast. It's a tidy town, with plane trees circling the square and pale stone buildings with white-washed shutters. The Mairie opposite is an elegant simple building with flower pots blooming at every window. A cat pads across the square and jumps up to drink at the fountain.

At La Caunette, a woman hangs her washing in the backyard to dry in the gathering breeze. It's a lovely village built into the side of a hill with stone and brick houses and shady alleyways. Swallows nest under the rafters of an abandoned shed, red-flowering creeper clings to the houses as if holding them together and a roadside cherry tree offers the last of its fruit to a grateful cyclist.

We crest a hill and look down into the canyon where the Cesse River flows. The next five kilometres are a treat as the road hugs the canyon wall following the river. It's wild and untamed, the perfect place for an ascetic and spartan religion to take root. We round one final bend and see Minerve, seemingly anchored and impregnable on an island in the canyon. The only entry is over the narrow and high-arched bridge. No vehicles, except those owned by residents, are allowed in a village that has been selected as *Les Plus Beaux Villages de France*, the most beautiful villages of France.

Suitably impressed, we walk the narrow laneways and marvel at the view down into the canyon. There are a few restaurants and tourist shops but unlike some similarly titled villages, Minerve is not overrun with tourists and garish tat. We sit in an outdoor cafe, drink a coffee and listen to the quiet.

Such was not the case in the Year 1210, when a band of Cathars fleeing the massacre in Beziers sought refuge in the town. The murderous Simon de Montfort, also responsible for the Bram massacre, laid siege to the town for six weeks, using four trebuchets to wreak terrible destruction. The town's water supply was cut off before a surrender was negotiated. The Cathars were given an ultimatum to renounce their faith and be guaranteed safe passage. Up to one hundred and forty Cathars refused and were burned at the stake. De Montfort razed the buildings. Only the octagonal tower remains from this bloodthirsty period.

I like Minerve, this cluster of old stone buildings marooned on a rock. It seems so isolated, yet is less than an hour by car to the Mediterranean.

We cross back over the three-arched bridge and cycle towards Aigne, enjoying the last kilometre downhill to the village which is laid out in an unusual spiral shape known as l'Escargot. No doubt this is for fortification purposes and it works a treat as we struggle to find the village centre! When we do, all the shops are closed and we weave our way back out of town, hungry and thirsty and pedalling furiously towards Bize in the hope that the Cafe Canal du Midi is still serving lunch.

We arrive back at 2:30 in the weary afternoon and the cafe is full... except for one vacant table. The waitress remembers us, even though we're dressed in garish lycra. She brings two jugs of cold water. The lunch special is a surprise. For nine Euro ninety centimes, we are each presented with a rectangular wicker tray of plates. On the biggest plate is the main course, a steak with roast potatoes. It's surrounded by smaller plates of:- a green salad; a wrap sandwich of jambon, fromage and salad; a thick wedge of cheese; and a crème brûlée. It's like a portable four-course picnic tray. It's washed down with a complimentary glass of wine. I look around the restaurant. Everyone from two old ladies at the table next to us to the group of eight hairy motorcyclists are tucking into the lunch. There are very few leftovers. It's a humourous, tasty version of the long French lunch. I'm pleased we came all the way back to Bize for lunch.

In the afternoon, with the sun at its hottest, we walk through the village and follow a dusty trail to the river where there's a narrow concrete bridge spanning the cool rushing water. We recline in the shade and I dip my hand in the river. I'm tempted to roll off the bridge into its bracing flow, but instead I doze the afternoon away.

For tonight, we have the arduous task of eating everything Dennis has prepared.

What a feast. I reassure Cathie that after all the kilometres we've cycled, we can indulge. We all gather at the long table in the garden. Dennis mentions that an American couple will also be joining us, but they're cycling from Sete and could be awhile. We drink a few beers while waiting. Then a few more more beers. Finally, Dennis relents and brings the bounty of food. Dear Reader, so as to not appear too indulgent, I will simply list the variety on offer. Salmon baked in the oven, Pork ribs with Dennis's 'special' sauce, grilled chicken thighs, sausages, roast duck and bowls of every salad imaginable. It feels like Christmas in June!

We eat and drink and tell stories. The Scots tell us about the wild pristine wilderness areas of the Highlands and we indulge with tales of animals in Australia that can kill people, everything from snakes to spiders to tiny jellyfish. The stories get more exaggerated as our stomachs expand, our glasses refill and the evening grows dark. Then the Americans arrive.

Dennis, the perfect host, has managed to snatch samples of each dish from our greedy hands. The evening tilts from stingrays in the Great Barrier Reef, deer in the roaming glen, to lawyers in Boston. We all know who are the most ferocious and deadly.

Accommodation: Maison des Palmiers, 12 Avenue de l'Amiral Narbonne, Bize-Minervois. Lovely hosts, wonderful breakfast, wifi, pool, outdoor dining, garage for bikes, peaceful village. Double E55-75, depending on choice of rooms, including breakfast. My score: 18/20.

Restaurant: Maison des Palmiers. If possible, spend a evening sharing dinner with Dennis and Hilary. They are gracious entertaining hosts and Dennis cooks a feast. Dinner E19, including wine. My score: 17/20.

Distance cycled: 38 km

What I should have said: 'What do you call a Scotsman at the World Cup? The referee.'

Chapter Twelve

Bize-Minervois to Beziers

I am a football tragic. The first time my son saw his father cry was when Australia surrendered a two goal lead in the final qualifying game for the 1998 World Cup Finals. Iran, our opponents that fateful evening in Melbourne, scored two late goals to progress on the away-goal rule. I sat on the back verandah and sobbed. It had been twenty-four years since we'd qualified for the finals. It would be another eight long years before we finally made it in 2006.

Today, back in Australia, the national team takes on Iraq in a do-or-die clash to progress to the finals in Brazil. Hilary and Dennis are kind enough to allow us a late check-out so I can sit entranced in the living room watching the game streamed live. For eighty-five torturous minutes, I cannot talk, as Australia attack the Iraqi goal in vain. Finally, with five minutes remaining, our tall striker, Josh Kennedy heads the winner and Dennis and Hilary witness the curious sight of a middle-aged man in lycra jumping around their living room. Cathie pretends not to notice as she reads a book in the garden.

Still high on adrenaline thirty minutes later, I cycle rapidly up the hill on the back road leading us to the Canal. Cathie cruises behind and admires the red dirt craggy hills and the Appaloosa horses roaming wild. When she finally catches up to me at the summit, she says simply, 'The game's over. We won.'

'How do you feel about cycling through Brazil next year,' I suggest.

'Let's make it to the Mediterranean first, shall we,' comes the taciturn reply.

It's downhill through vineyards all the way to the Canal and after two days away from the channel, I'm once again immediately struck by how beautiful the plane trees are. The streaming shafts of light, the falling leaves, the dappled water. Magic.

Unfortunately, the track has not improved in quality. In fact, parts are so overgrown as to be non-existent. We round a bend and cycle into a swarm of midges. Cough cough goes the husband, splutter splutter goes the wife. It only lasts for a minute, but we both reach for the water bottles to drench our faces and wash the midges from our eyes and nasal passages. I snort water up my nose in a successful if tear-inducing bid to remove the last remaining insects.

We decide to take the upper path on the right bank and are treated to a lovely vista over vineyards down to a distant village. An iron cross stands beside the path, but I can see no inscriptions as to its purpose.

Capestang has an imposing cathedral that can be seen for miles around, dwarfing the surrounding buildings. The Collegiate St-Etienne dates from the 13th century and is under the control of the Archbishop of Narbonne. Unfortunately, it's closed when we arrive as are the two boulangeries. The only open shops are two bars opposite each other on the square. Men sit at outside tables of each bar, staring blankly across the park at their comrades. I wonder what all the women of the town are doing?

We cycle to the Malpas tunnel, one of the major works of the canal. At one hundred and seventy metres long and seven metres high, Pierre Paul Riquet began work on its construction without the approval of the King. Realising he had to work quickly, his workers completed the tunnelling in only eight days, just before the order was announced for all work to cease.

We walk down the steep rough-hewn stone steps to peer into the tunnel. The roof is hard packed dirt, pockmarked with what I imagine are holes for the resident bat population. There's a narrow path for walkers through the tunnel and we wait beside a gaggle of tourists, all with cameras at the ready, for the next barge to approach. The Captain of the vessel seems to sit up that little bit straighter as he has his photo taken by all of us, just at the point where the boat enters the dark tunnel. His wife permits herself a shy wave.

Back on high ground above the tunnel, we climb the steep road on the left bank which affords us a lovely view of the Etang de Montady, a drained lake. In the 12th century, the area was a wetlands reserve until the local monks came up with an ingenious plan to drain the lake. They dug radial ditches that spiralled into a central culvert where the water was then drained under the Malpas hill. To this day, the field plots are of a triangular shape due to the radial drains. It's a curious sight from high above, a formal wheel of vineyards and orchards seeming to flow into a central hub.

At nearby Columbiers, we cross the a hump-backed bridge dating from Riquet's period and are met with a scowl from the driver of an oversized utility. He apparently considers his bulk has right of way over two good-natured cyclists. He winds down his window and spits something in French. I don't think it's 'have a nice day.' I permit myself a knowing smirk. It seems the world over is populated by hostile men driving utility vehicles. Maybe before they're allowed to buy one, they have to sit an 'angry test.' Only the most irrational drivers are allowed to purchase these oversized boys toys. I wave to him, although I'm sorely tempted to blow him a kiss.

We each purchase a delicious tarte pomme from the boulangerie near the lovely St Sylvestre church. Then it's back over the bridge and along the canal where a group of much happier men spend the afternoon playing boules.

We dodge numerous exposed roots along the path but I reason where there's roots, there's majestic plane trees. In the gathering gloom of the afternoon, the trees cast an ominous light over the canal. I feel as though I'm riding through a gothic novel. The water looks black and oily, the sky a bruised purple, the leaves fall silently to the ground and I half-expect a cloaked madman to spring from behind the bushes, a sabre in his hand.

Instead, a child rolls a football playfully along the path.

Just before Beziers, we arrive at the astounding Fonserannes locks. These eight locks form a water staircase for barges, allowing the water level to rise by an impressive twenty-two metres. It's a staggering example of early engineering. Cathie and I lean our bikes against a fence and join the hundreds of people watching the barges slowly climb the staircase. Yes, hundreds of people come every day to view the spectacle.

It dawns on me that we are here in the 21st century, with our modern smartphones taking photos and videos and staring open-mouthed in wonder at an invention of the 17th century. As our precious planet and ecosystem reels under the man-made effects of climate change, I can't help but wonder what a visionary like Pierre Paul Riquet would make of our collective selfishness and disorder?

The captains of the three rising barges work feverishly in each lock chambre, not because they have that much actual work to do, but they do have an audience of hundreds. Orders are called to willing second mates and fingers are pointed where to steer, all with a knowing smile for the cameras. The tourist shops and restaurants are doing a roaring trade and the ghost of Riquet smiles down upon Fonserannes.

Beziers in the birthplace of Riquet, but with new roadworks, it's not a welcoming town for cyclists. We weave in between a kilometre-long traffic jam (or as I prefer to call it, *a confiture de traffic*) before staggering up a very steep hill to finally reach a statue of the great man in the town square, surrounded with a lovely flowerbed near the appropriately named Jardins du Plateau des Poetes.

I resist the urge to tell Cathie that I'm in the garden of the poets, where I belong.

A brief aside while I mention that in the past week I've received pleasing news that my latest book, a verse-novel for children, has been shortlisted for five major literary awards in Australia. Surely, I can claim the mantle of *a poet* now. Or should I wait until the winners are announced?

Beziers has a turbulent history with perhaps the worst day being the 22nd of July, 1209 when the twenty thousand inhabitants were massacred in the Crusades. The town sank into obscurity for centuries after, only to be revived by the burgeoning wine trade at the beginning of the 20th century. Today, Beziers is a bustling multicultural town of kebab and pizza shops and men puffing on pipes in smoky cafes.

We check into our hotel opposite the statue of Pierre Paul Riquet, to be greeted by a smiling receptionist who doesn't speak a word of English. Cue five minutes of animated mime as she describes where I have to carry the bikes for storage. Up a steep flight of stairs, behind a rope-lined hallway, past a curtain and... voila! Craig and Jenny squeeze into the tight space and I wish them good night. The woman wonders why I'm talking to the bicycles.

She's a friendly soul who smilingly gives us a choice of rooms, front or side of hotel? We choose the side room with a tiny balcony overlooking a kebab shop. The smells waft through our open door.

In the early evening, we wander the streets, admiring the imposing St Nazaire Cathedral that dominates the skyline. Over the entrance door is a wood carving of a beheading that represents the martyrdom of St Nazaire. Near the Cathedral is the Place des Bon Amis where four leaders of the revolt against the Duke of Berry were beheaded.

Enough bloodthirsty history. It's time to eat dinner. I hope the steak is well cooked.

Accommodation: Hotel Paul Riquet, 1 rue Victor Hugo, Beziers. Friendly staff, great location, small room, wifi, (tight) storage for bicycles. Double E55, breakfast extra. My score: 15/20

Restaurant: Brasserie le Victor, 31 Place Jean Jaures. We are greeted at the entrance by a brown-eyed young waitress wearing tight jeans and a swinging cardigan who directs us to a table inside, away from the smokers.

Surely one of the delights of French life is the chance to indulge in an aperitif in the evening at an outdoor table, watching the world go by. But one of the most annoying things in French society is the number of people who smoke at these very same outdoor tables? Call me a prude, but I don't want to drink and eat through a fug of smelly health-threatening smoke.

Back to the rather haughty but charming waitress and our indoor table. She reels off the formule menu with a characteristic 'a' sound at the end of many words, a regional trait I'm told. We order salade au chevre (pronounced *chevra*) chaud, a barely-cooked slice of boeuf with frites and a Creme de Marrons Chantilly. It's all tasty and well-prepared, although I have difficulty eating the steak after talk of so many beheadings. It's an atmospheric casual restaurant that I'd recommend. Bring a gas mask and enjoy the early evening at an outdoor table. Formule menu E15.80. My score: 16/20

Distance cycled: 47 km

Actual distance: 42 km

What I should have said: 'It's okay, Craig. There are no ghosts in the attic. Believe me.'

Chapter Thirteen

Beziers to Sete

We begin today with breakfast at a cafe on the square. At this early hour, it's full of men in fluorescent work vests and office workers grabbing a coffee and croissant on the go. We eat a croissant and a slice of baguette smeared with jam, washed down with coffee from an automatic machine, before facing the surging traffic heading downhill. Craig finds the steep road almost as scary as the dark attic, but manfully survives both with barely a whimper. His rider makes enough fearful noises for both of them.

Safely back on the canal, it's tree root obstacle time. Bumpity bump bump clang bump.

Oh stop it! Stop harping on how in the 17th century they can build a canal so majestic and awe-inspiring that four centuries later, people still throng to gaze at its wonders. And yet, here in the 21st century, we can't bitumen a metre-wide path to allow us to enjoy such ancient wonders as the Malpas Tunnel and the Fonserannes locks. Riquet built engineering masterpieces, not towpaths.

As if hearing my complaints, at the next bend the canal path widens and is paved. Merci! A sign on the stone wall announces the imminent arrival in Beziers of a famous lounge singer.

'I'd like to be a chassures francaise,' I say.

'I think you mean chanson,' says my erudite wife, 'although a *french shoe* perhaps sums up your singing style.'

We cycle alongside swampy fields of a shallow lagoon with long-legged birds wading in the marshes. Near the Beziers port, there's a fenced prison for hundreds of disused canal bikes, waiting repair or the scrap heap. Craig curses to see so many of his comrades locked up, going nowhere, covered in plastic tarps, seats removed, tyres flat.

At Libron, we cross the gates erected in 1855 to regulate the flow of the river over the canal in times of extreme flooding. It's a complex maze of rusting gadgetry that I'm afraid I can't understand. Craig, perhaps upset at the bicycle prison, begins changing gear when he shouldn't.

Oh dear.

If I can't fathom the workings of an 1855 mechanical gate, what hope do I have with 21st century bicycle gearing? I make a slight adjustment and... miraculously it's fixed. For our last day on the canal, Craig finally makes things just that little bit easier.

We detour to Vias, a fortified village built in the 12th century, that nows seems more beach resort than bastide. There's a market in full swing at the Centre Ville and we nervously wheel our bikes through the crowds searching for the most popular boulangerie. Two almond croissants later, it's back along the busy beach road to the canal.

And so to Agde and the only round lock on the canal. The lock has three exits: to the canal back towards Vias, to the Herault River, and to a small canal that runs into Agde. We detour into the village and witness a rasta-haired man on an old bicycle riding down the main street in the centre of the lane. Despite his dawdling pace, no-one sounds their horn or tries to overtake. He looks very wild and intimidating. Cathie and I follow meekly behind, well off to the right.

The towpath disappears and we cyclists are forced to brave the rigours of the D51 to Marseillan. In fact, every guide book I've read now advises us to ignore the canal and its non-existent path and follow back roads to near the mouth at the Bassin de Thau.

After over seven hundred and seventy kilometres of joyous cycling along the two canals and through the surrounding countryside, it's hugely disappointing to not be able to spend the final ten kilometres cycling alongside the canal.

Instead, we cycle past a rubbish dump, a few disused buildings and a lonely factory before the back road peters out entirely. Ahead of us is a dirt track through a vineyard. Cathie and I look at each other and shrug in tandem. What the heck. We slowly ride along the path, enjoying the serenity of the vineyard and wondering where we'll end up. Incongruously, after a few kilometres, we arrive at the fag-end of a new housing estate. We have no idea where the canal is. Or, in fact, where we are. Accompanied by a sea breeze and the barking of a score of neighbourhood dogs, we finally reach a brand spanking new cycle path.

'Look, Craig,' I shout, 'pavement!'

This treat lasts for precisely one kilometre before a bridge announces our final meeting with the canal.

From the location where Cathie and Jenny and Craig and I now proudly stand, the canal empties into the Bassin less than five hundred metres away. But there is no path, no dirt track, no way that we can cycle to the mouth.

'Seven hundred and seventy kilometres!' I shout to the canal water. In vain.

We both sigh and take the obligatory photos beside the canal.

Look, everyone. There's the mouth... over there, in the distance. Pah!

'We could walk it,' Cathie says, before answering herself, 'but it won't be the same without Craig and Jenny.'

'I'm not leaving Craig,' I answer.

Sadly we wave goodbye to the Canal du Midi, and by extension, the Canal de Garonne and twelve days of cycling through an ever-changing landscape. The Riquet masterpiece built by twelve thousand men and women who dug the canal, erected bridges, aqueducts, sixty-two ovoid-shaped locks and the single round lock at Agde, before filling it with water and barges, now silently flows unaccompanied into the Bassin de Thau. Unaccompanied, but not unloved.

Our journey does not finish here. Sete is twelve kilometres along the coast. It's early afternoon and we haven't had lunch, so I propose a celebratory meal by the sea which is somewhere south of here.

As if to ease our disappointment, the path to Sete is a beauty. It's apparent a considerable amount of money has gone into restoring the old beachfront road into a cycle path through the dunes. The wind whips off the Mediterranean at a comfortable angle over our right shoulder, pushing us towards Sete. I ride with one casual hand steering, waving the other at the magnificent vista of sea and sand and dogs chasing frisbees thrown by holidaymakers. What is it about beaches that encourage we adults to be children again?

To our right is the Mediterranean, to our left are holiday parks of various shades of wealth: from well organised and arranged parks of neat cabins and jaunty timber shacks to down-at-heel leftovers from decades past. There are wind-blown fences everywhere in a vain attempt to contain the shifting sands and promote growth of the native vegetation. It's too early in the season for many restaurants to bother opening, so we continue our push into Sete.

As if approaching Shangri la, our eyes scan the eastern horizon. I haven't read anything about the town of Sete, but expect it to be a cramped and overcrowded European beach resort. Sorry, we Australians, with our excess miles of white sandy beaches, can be a little snobby about the European variety.

Just to prove me wrong, Sete arrives with a lovely promenade of palm trees and modern well-designed low-rise apartment blocks, each with a restaurant or cafe at the front.

'Traditional three course indulgence, with wine?' I suggest to Cathie.

She shakes her head, pointing instead to a lovely cafe under the palm trees serving galettes.

'It's not Brittany, but...' she says.

We lean Craig and Jenny against a palm tree, as if symbolising the end of their journey. From plane tree to palm tree. The well-dressed waiter smiles while I take a photo of our two hard-working steeds. We order two ciders and two galettes with jambon, fromage and a runny ouef on top.

We lean back in the well-padded seats and toast our bicycles, each other, the sea, but most of all, the Canals des Deux Mers for their seven hundred and seventy kilometres of friendship and direction.

'We've done it,' I say, perhaps unnecessarily.

I am immensely proud of my beautiful wife. From belly dancer to bicyclist in twelve days!

The galettes are excellent, as is the Brittany cider. I don't really want to leave this glorious vista, but Sete awaits. What a surprise is in store. Sete is a truly beautiful seaside resort town, better than any in Australia. There, I said it!

Yes, it must bear the burden of the ludicrous 'Venice of the South' tag, but ignore that. It's a working sea port that has maintained its character, history and age-old opulence without becoming horrendously exclusive and elite. Perhaps the smell of fish scares off the extravagantly wealthy, leaving this pearl for the rest of us.

Cathie and I cycle over the hill towards town with a sea mist cloaking the horizon. Despite the cool breeze, couples are out strolling the promenade, families eat gelato in cafes and the ever-present French old lady walks her treasured chein.

Downhill and a sharp left turn, through a roundabout or two, and the port opens up in the afternoon sunshine. Large fishing boats are moored three deep in sections of the channel, with an endless parade of seafood restaurants lining either side. Despite the traffic and the crowds, it doesn't feel cluttered, just happily busy and alive. A real town not a holiday enclave. We ride the streets, marvelling at the canals and the old buildings artfully restored. There's a beautiful ornate cafe on one corner and two doors down from this gem on a back street is our hotel. The friendly chap at reception shows us where to leave Craig and Jenny. No tacky garage for these long-distance angels. They stay the night in air-conditioned comfort under the stairs near the lobby, snug and secure. Craig nudges close to Jenny. Ah, young love.

Our room is large and simple and we set about washing our lycra for the last time on this journey. It's almost fun.

Laundry finished, we wander the streets of the port. The mist has blown away and the sun shines brightly, as if on cue. Sete is the birthplace of the poet Paul Valery. I'm trying to think of a better place for a poet to be born. There's something about the atmosphere and unpredictability of a working port or harbour. It's why modern politicians build glass and concrete capital cities as far away from the ocean as possible. Witness Brasilia in preference to Rio de Janeiro or our very own Canberra instead of Sydney or Melbourne. Ports are places for humans with all their foibles and eccentricities.

We take a seat at the Restaurant Marie-Jean, suggested by the chap at reception. It's one of the many restaurants along the Canal de Sete where the large fishing boats are moored for the evening. Not surprisingly, seafood features prominently on the menu. My entree of mussels are stacked to overflowing in the bowl and are meaty and salty in equal measures. I have swordfish, cooked in butter, accompanied by potatoes for main course and finish with a simple delicious fromage blanc for dessert. All washed down with the obligatory pichet de rosé.

Afterwards, we stroll along the quay in the fading light, holding hands.

'Maybe we should cycle down the Danube next year,' Cathie says as we cross the Pont de la Savonnerie.

It's one reason why I love her.

We rush back to the hotel to tell Craig and Jenny the good news.

Accommodation: Le National Hotel, 2 rue Pons De L'herault, Sete. Friendly staff, wifi, storage for bicycles, large simple rooms, close to the the centre of town and train station, yet in a quiet location. Double E70, breakfast extra. My score: 15/20.

Restaurant: Restaurant Le Marie-Jean, 26 Quai General Durand, Sete. Excellent location, good value, simple tasty seafood. Formule menu E16.50 My score: 16/20.

Distance cycled: 60 km
Actual distance: 51 km
What I should have said: 'Au revoir mon canal, adieu...'

Chapter Fourteen

Col de Peyresourde

Those of you who have read *baguettes and bicycles*, my previous book on cycling in France will know that I enjoy the occasional cycle up a very steep mountain. Let me hastily assure you this has nothing whatsoever to do with testosterone and macho posturing. Being from the flattest continent on Earth, I simply love the unparalleled scenery of European mountains and a bicycle is the slowest and most evocative way to experience these natural marvels.

In 2012, I cycled up quite a few of the iconic Tour de France Alps, including Alpe d'Huez, Col du Galibier and the awe-inspiring Col de la Croix der Fer. It was an experience I'll never forget. I quickly became addicted to the long slow grind uphill. I found it curiously meditative. With nothing to do but pedal slowly and enjoy the scenery, my heart rate slowed and my mind cleared. Who needs a tai chi class when you have a mountain to climb?

There is certainly a sense of achievement on getting to the summit under my own steam, but that isn't the primary motivation. I am simply in awe of where a bicycle can take an ordinary chap. The most wonderful invention deserves to share in the most majestic scenery.

Unfortunately, I cannot convince Cathie of the attraction.

Over dinner in Sete, we planned our following week. The conversation went something like this.

'So, how far do you reckon the Pyrenees are from here,' I asked nervously.

'Wouldn't it be lovely to spend a week on the beach,' she replied, ignoring my clumsy hint.

Silence.

'Let's check the weather forecast, shall we,' Cathie said.

After an unseemly rush to the mobile phone, I was 'rewarded' with a forecast of dull skies and showers for the next five days.

'Okay, I'll walk in the mountains while you do your impression of a monk on a bicycle,' Cathie smiled.

In the end, we compromised. Five days in the mountains, followed by time spent on a beach. Perfect! We both agreed that with all the exercise of riding and walking in the mountains, at least we could eat and drink to excess in the evenings, knowing the next day brought even more climbing and walking. Well, that was our excuse.

I have read as much literature as I can find on the Pyrenees climbs and have decided on attempting the three most iconic mountains. The Col de Peyresourde, Col d'Aubisque and the legendary Col de Tourmalet. If my knees don't creak to a halt, I have three days of slow uphills and teeth-gritting downhills to enjoy.

We arrive in the spa town of Bagnere-de-Luchon in the afternoon. The sun is out, casually disregarding the bleak weather forecast. It's a lovely old town with a wide main street and elegant cafes and boulangeries. The holiday groups appear to be either pensioners here to soak in the recuperative powers of the hot springs or lycra-clad cyclists here to climb the surrounding peaks. Not far from the hot baths, our hotel is a wonderful example of faded but still regal spa town accommodation, with chandeliers in the lovely dining room where well-dressed guests are served by formally-attired waiters. It's not normally our style, but we got a very good deal on a booking web-site and I figure my long-suffering wife deserves all the pampering we can afford.

I'm so excited about beginning my adventure that I go in search of an open bike shop in the hope of renting a carbon-fibre bike to climb the mountains. Craig deserves a rest. The first shop I locate looks more like a cycle cemetery with bike parts and worn tyres scattered around the entrance. There are numerous second-hand bikes for sale. They all look rather creaky and sad. The owner comes out of his workshop and nods hello.

I ask to hire a 'velo pour le montagnes.' My grammar is like my cycling, shaky at the best of the times. The owner surveys the mess of his workshop and walks across to a black carbon-fibre model that looks sturdy yet well-used. I ask him the price. Usual daily rental cost is somewhere between thirty and forty-five euros.

He says, 'Fifteen euros.'

I nod uncertainly, trying to hide my excitement.

'Avez vous pump, repair kit,' I say, mixing bad French with lazy English. He shrugs but I think it means yes.

I rush back to the hotel, change into lycra, scoff a cake Cathie has thoughtfully bought me and quickly return to the bike shop where the owner takes my credit card and fifteen euros. With some sluggishness, he lowers my seat, pumps the tyres and fits a repair kit. I ask to fill my water bottle. He says he has no water and I should go to the cemetery around the corner. From one cemetery to the other, I think.

Although it's now late in the afternoon, I'm aware I have at least five hours of daylight left with darkness not arriving until ten in the evening. Surely even at my slow pace, I can climb Col de Peyresourde in that time?

Col de Peyresourde is a mountain pass in the Central Pyrenees that forms the border between Haute-Garonne and Haute-Pyrenees. The road across is the legendary D918 (more about this mecca for cyclists later) between Luchon and Arreau.

Peyresourde is used frequently by the Tour de France. Last count, fifty-five times, beginning in 1910. In fact, it was ridden twice in 2012 and will, hopefully, be traversed again in 2013. I say 'hopefully' because last week, Luchon was inundated in a terrible flood caused by excessive rain and the accompanying snow melt. There are photos of the water, sixty centimetres deep on the road, swirling past the hotel where we are staying. Parts of the town are still covered in layers of mud, turning to dust in the sun.

I set off and it's immediately apparent that the seat position is too far back. I can barely reach the handlebars. I return to my new friend and he reluctantly moves the seat forward and gives it one desultory slap to straighten it. What can I expect for fifteen euros.

I have christened the bike, Murray. The brand name is Massi, reputedly from Italy by way of the USA. So if Murray is confused about his heritage, giving him a sturdy and sensible moniker can only help. Murray and I take the first roundabout and stop at the cemetery. I fill my water bottle and gaze respectfully at the rows of graves.

The first few kilometres of the climb are around 6-8% gradient, with a forest and rushing stream as a relaxing vista.

A few weeks before Cathie and I cycled the canals, Craig and I climbed the Passo Dello Stelvio, the second highest mountain pass in the European Alps. It was slow going. In contrast to Craig, Murray feels like a racehorse, although he has a nasty tendency to change gear unexpectedly. My knees are not enjoying his tricky surprises, so I attempt something I hate doing. I adjust the gears. And voila, it's fixed. Perhaps my friend in the bike cemetery would be proud of me?

Murray responds and we cruise into the first village. Like many Pyrenean hamlets, it's a collection of dour grey stone houses that look as if the residents have permanently bunkered down. Surprisingly as the afternoon wears on, the wispy clouds disappear and the temperature warms. Summer appears to have arrived. It's twenty-two degrees and climbing much faster than we cyclists. So much for the reliability of weather forecasts.

The first church is a beauty, nestled into the hill with green meadows rising steeply behind it and a cemetery of statues and stone near the entrance.

There are a few cyclists out this afternoon and surprisingly Murray seems to be passing them. The are all wearing *Carcassonne* jerseys, so I assume the riders are used to the flatlands of the Canal du Midi. Two cyclists have stopped ahead and are taking turns to dunk their heads under a fountain. I stop and fill my water bottle. I love a mountain that allows you to climb it and supplies you with cold clean drinking water.

After ten kilometres the road opens out with glorious views across the valley to a village halfway up a steep slope. Beside the road, hang-gliders prepare to take off, but unfortunately I can't stop to watch. Murray has rhythm and he won't be denied.

To add to the lovely ambience of a stunning mountain, cowbells begin ringing. A herd below me casually graze on the thick green grass and play music. Off to my right in the distance are snow-capped mountains, but I'm surprised by how little snow there is on the surrounding peaks. Sadly, much of it became floodwater that ravaged the villages below.

I'm on the final three kilometres now and the hairpins are coming steep and sharp. I love how the French use the word 'lacet' to describe hairpin bends. Shoelaces. There is a group of cyclists above me, shouting encouragement down to their comrades from Carcassonne. A cyclist just ahead of me is blowing hard, I can hear him from five metres back. I pass and wish him 'bonne courage.' He puffs in answer.

I pull out to pass another cyclist, a heavy-set man wearing a bandanna. I nod hello. He grins and in mock anguish, reaches out towards the summit, pleading 'le montagne, le montagne.' I can't help but smile. As I pass his comrades waiting up ahead, they stand as one to cheer him on. They look to be having the time of their lives.

Two more lacets and the summit arrives much earlier than I expected. My Garmin says I still have a kilometre to climb, but I'm not arguing with the Col de Peyresourde sign that I dutifully stand in front of while a fellow cyclist snaps my photo. We both head to the cafe, he to join his mates, me to order a soft drink. I'd love a cider but the thought of descending on the unpredictable Murray stays my hand. I sit in the sun and contemplate the cafe special, fifty-centime crepes. Cheap tasty crepes eaten in the most beautiful scenery. A just reward.

The descent is cold but invigorating. There is little traffic and as the evening chill takes hold, fewer cyclists. I prefer climbing than descending. There is nothing meditative about gripping the brakes as I rip around a corner at the edge of my abilities. I try to go as slow as possible and enjoy the views but Murray is light and efficient and wants to streak ahead. The descent is when I miss Craig. He knows how to relax.

I arrive back in Luchon with enough time for a quick shower before dinner. Although the restaurant looks much too elegant for our taste, we've decided to splurge. Surprisingly, the cost for a formule three-course menu is a very agreeable nineteen euros, fifty centimes. And what an excellent meal it is. For entree, we both choose the chevre fromage wrapped in grilled aubergines and courgettes with a coulis of red peppers. It's superb. The genial waiter keeps returning, asking if we'd like wine. He can't understand why we uncivilised Australians are content to drink beer with our meal. For main course, Cathie has the baked whole trout sprinkled with almond slivers. I choose my usual, confit de canard. Both dishes are perfectly cooked.

We are already deciding what we'll order tomorrow night when dessert arrives. We both chose the same dish, although we had no idea what it was. On each plate are long fluted donuts similar to Spanish churros, accompanied by prunes and armagnac ice cream. They are divine. We cannot believe we are eating so well, so cheaply.

I can't wait to climb Col du Tourmalet tomorrow... and to return here in the evening. As we leave, we make a booking for the same table.

Col de Peyresourde is a hors category climb of sixteen kilometres, with an average gradient of 6.6% and a maximum gradient of 10%. The altitude is 1589 metres with an elevation gain of 944 metres when climbed from the Luchon side. The Col links the Aure and Louron valleys.

Accommodation: Hotel d'Etigny, 3 Ave Paul Bonnemaison, Luchon. Friendly hosts, good comfortable rooms, wifi (best reception in the lobby), good value, if you can get a special deal. Excellent dinner but an average breakfast. Double 48 Euros, breakfast extra. My score: 16/20

Restaurant: Hotel d'Etigny, 3 Ave Paul Bonnemaison, Luchon. Friendly knowledgeable waiters, superb food and excellent value when choosing from the formule menu, elegant setting, see my review above. My score: 18/20

Distance cycled: 32 km

What I should have said: 'But, Monsieur, of course all Australians drink beer with dinner. C'est natural!'

Chapter Fifteen

Col du Tourmalet

Surprisingly, the breakfast in the same elegant dining room is a disappointment. The well-dressed waiters of last night are replaced with one friendly but overworked young woman who rushes between tables filling coffee cups. The croissants and bread rolls look generic and taste stale and the jam comes in individual foil sachets.

I'm still looking forward to tonight's dinner though.

In 2010, I drove a car half-way up Col du Tourmalet in the French Pyrenees. It was a bleak misty and rainy day, with the wind blowing a gale. I parked by the side of the road and opened the car door. The wind nearly blew it from its hinges. I scrambled out and took photos of myself, the fool in the mist. I got back in the car, where my wife and our friends all agreed we should head back down the mountain. As I reversed out of the car park, four cyclists rode past us, up the hill into the tumult. What I was scared to attempt in a car, they were doing on bicycles. I looked up towards the summit shrouded in cloud and wanted to follow this strange band of hardy lycra-wearing crazies.

Today, in Sainte-Marie-de-Campan, I have my chance. I'm about to climb one of the most revered and feared climbs of the Tour de France. Not from the side I'd driven up in 2010, because it's still closed due to recent flooding. I'm climbing the equally-difficult east side. It was from this side in 1913, where Eugene Christophe broke his fork on Tourmalet and repaired it himself in Sainte-Marie after carrying the bike for hours down the mountain. He was subsequently disqualified because he'd allowed a young man to work the bellows as he repaired the fork. This counted as 'outside assistance.'

I could use some of that myself as I begin the journey out from Sainte-Marie-de-Campan. I'm tremendously excited to be climbing

Tourmalet because, if I reach the summit, it will complete my ascent of the big four of the Tour de France - Alpe d'Huez; Col de Galibier and Mont Ventoux being the others. On each of these climbs, I've been fortunate to have clear skies and mild temperatures. Today is no exception. There's even a wind at my back. And a group of British and American cyclists. A few overtake me in the first kilometre, setting a cracking pace. I dawdle along at my usual relaxed doddle, checking my heart rate on the Garmin. Below 150, which I try to maintain as the gradient cranks up a few percentage points.

I'm surprised by the relative ease of the first few kilometres as it meanders through a stretch of rural houses, each with a garden and a resident chien. The gradient increases as I enter a forest section with storming waterfalls flowing under the road at strategic bridges. At every kilometre, there's a sign that let's me know how far to the summit and the average gradient for the next kilometre. Painfully, ten kilometres from the peak, I am facing a stiff 8.5% climb. Ouch. What was that about an easy start.

A lone cyclist has been drafting me for the last few minutes. I don't mind helping someone up this fearsome stretch. But of course, when he passes, he gestures for me to tuck in him behind him.

'We help each other,' he says, in French-accented English.

It's what I've been dreading. I hate drafting for two reasons. Firstly, I always struggle to keep up the pace. Secondly, I don't really want to be staring at the back wheel of a bicycle the whole way up Tourmalet. I'm not here to climb the mountain quickly. I just want to relax. But how can I explain that as the cyclist slows to let me catch up.

'Non, merci,' I bleat, hoping he'll understand.

He cordially waves a hand and increases his speed, soon disappearing around the next bend.

I take one hand off the handlebar and stretch out in my seat, relaxed once again. I think of everything I've read of this legendary mountain. Perhaps my favourite story is of Alphonse Steines, who originally scouted the climb prior to the 1910 Tour to see whether it was suitable to be crossed by bicycles. He drove half-way up the mountain, then started walking before getting totally lost, falling in a stream, slipping on the ice and finally being rescued by a search party sent from Barages. When he was safely back at the hotel, he sent a telegraph to Henri Desgranges, the Tour organiser, which read, 'Crossed Tourmalet stop. Very good road stop. Perfectly feasible.'

The legend of the mountain was born soon after when the first rider over the summit in 1910, Octave Lapize is alleged to have shouted, 'Assassins' in the face of Tour officials.

I smile, remembering being afraid to drive a car up here three years ago. Since 1910, Tourmalet has been climbed more than any other mountain pass in the Tour, its status assured. It's part of the so-called 'circle of death' which includes Peyresourde, Col d'Aspin, Tourmalet and Col d'Aubisque, all able to be ridden in one day along the iconic D918 in perhaps the most epic stage of the Tour. I drove over Col d'Aspin to reach Sainte-Marie. It's a beautiful mountain. I'm tempted to ride it tomorrow. But all four mountains in the one day? *Assassins*, indeed.

For the rest of the climb the average doesn't drop below 8%. After a rather downtrodden caravan park, the road opens up and provides me with lovely views to the distant peaks, many covered in cloud, despite the sparkling day down here. I cycle through a number of long galleries, designed to prevent snow from covering the road. The road surface is very patchy and I think of what untold damage has been done to the other side in recent floods. Word is that route will be closed for months.

Four kilometres from the summit, when I'm feeling excited and entranced by the spectacular views, La Mongie hoves into sight. A ski resort by name, a monstrosity by nature. The first building is seven storeys high, the lower three levels are enclosed concrete which I imagine is for a car park. It's Le Corbusier ugliness is writ large in front of majestic snow-capped mountains. Further on up the village, which is a steep 8% gradient, is another resort, marginally less ugly but still in need of a crate of dynamite. As if to symbolise this horror, the road which has only been open a few weeks is caked in dried cow dung. La Mongie stinks. Appropriately.

Once free of this nastiness, the last four kilometres are absolutely divine. The gradient doesn't relent but the view of snow drifts, mountains, cows (with cow bells!) and craggy peaks is mind-boggling. At one point, I pass a tractor still clearing the road of snow and grit. He turns and slowly chases me up the hill. It's all I can do to keep ahead of him before he reaches the tip-truck to dump his load. Now that's one incentive to climb faster!

I reach the summit. The sun is shining, the view is spectacular and cyclists are crowding together shaking hands in congratulations. One cyclist lifts his bike above his head in exultation as his photo is taken in front of the altitude sign. I couldn't lift Murray if I tried, so I wheel him into frame and smile. The summit of Tourmalet is very small. The road reaches the peak and then drops immediately to the other side which is still closed. I gaze down the valley to where I'd driven last year. Ha!

Confusingly, the sculpture of the *giant of Tourmalet* is missing from his usual place cycling atop the rock wall at the summit. I'd been eager to get a photo in front of his contorted face. I expected his visage to mirror mine after all those kilometres. I'm told the giant is still in his winter home at Tarbes, even though it's June.

I walk to the edge of the dirt to look down at the other side, still blocked. Snowdrifts crowd the curling road. Further down, near Barages, there is no road left at all.

There's only one shop open up here, selling Tourmalet jerseys and souvenirs. I look longingly back towards Luz Saint Sauveur on the western side before putting on my jacket and respectfully nodding at the Pic du Midi peak which towers above Tourmalet.

The descent is extremely chilly and I stop at La Mongie for the only good thing in town. A donkey. Yes, standing in the middle of the road is a small, very hairy donkey. He looks at me and I look at him, neither moving for a minute. Then he walks casually towards me and accepts a pat and a rub on the neck. What a lovely chap. I'd vote him Mayor of La Mongie. He's got to be better than the ass who allowed this landscape to be so disfigured.

After a soft drink and a farewell pat, it's downhill all the way, bouncing through the gloomy galleries and dodging corners strewn with gravel. In the middle of the day, the road is lined with cyclists climbing, their faces contorted, like the Giant, their eyes hopefully set on the road ahead. I'm tempted to call, 'watch out for the donkey,' but I guess they'll see him holding court at La Mongie.

On the most feared climb of the Pyrenees, I have made a new friend.

Col du Tourmalet is a hors category climb, beginning in Sainte-Marie-de-Campan, of 17.2 kilometres with an average gradient of 7.4% and a maximum gradient of 10%. The elevation gain is 1,268 metres. It was the first mountain pass with an elevation of over 2,000 metres to be climbed by the Tour in 1910.

Accommodation: Hotel d'Etigny, 3 Ave Paul Bonnemaison, Luchon. Friendly hosts, good comfortable rooms, wifi (best reception in the lobby), good value, if you can get a special deal. Excellent dinner but an average breakfast. Double 48 euros, breakfast extra. My score: 16/20

Restaurant: Hotel d'Etigny, 3 Ave Paul Bonnemaison, Luchon. We're the first seated tonight, so eager are we to eat here again. The chef does not disappoint.

Friendly knowledgeable waiters, superb food and excellent value when choosing from the formule menu, elegant setting. Formule menu E19.50 My score: 18/20

Distance cycled: 35 km

What I should have said: 'Monsieur, I'll buy one Tourmalet jersey and one crate of dynamite for La Mongie, s'il vous plait.'

Chapter Sixteen

Col d'Aspin

The Col d'Aspin has featured sixty-six times in the Tour de France and yet is relatively unknown alongside its more prominent Pyrenees partners such as Tourmalet, Peyresourde and Superbagneres. Perhaps it's the relatively 'minor' altitude of 1,489 metres that sees it literally and metaphorically dwarfed against the Pyrenean giants. This is a pity. Col d'Aspin is truly one of the great mountain climbs of the Tour de France.

Avoiding the hotel breakfast, I stop at a boulangerie on the outskirts of Luchon. It's a bright sunny day and the lone baker happily makes me an excellent petit dejeuner. We have a misunderstanding about the coffee I've ordered, so he readily agrees to drink 'the mistake' himself while making me another one. Such a positive friendly man.

After a quick drive over Peyresourde to the village of Arreau, I begin my ascent of the eastern side of Aspin. It's still early in the morning, far too early for any self-respecting French cyclist. Consequently, I have the road to myself. Despite the sun, it's only nine degrees as I set out and Aspin offers me an easy warm-up with the first few kilometres averaging 4% among the forest beside a rushing stream. The road is much narrower than many Tour climbs and has lovely old stone walls as embankments. I quickly realise I am climbing an historic road, first used in the Tour in 1910.

The gradient soon cranks up and I'm amazed at the splendid views back to the snow-capped mountains on the Spanish border. They seem to loom larger as I climb. As I look ahead, I can see the pass where this road slips between two mountains. There appears to be animals grazing where the road should be but perhaps my eyes are playing tricks?

A man walks home from his morning stroll and enters a stone

farmhouse with a 180-degree view of stunning peaks. I wonder how much he wants for the old pile?

My climb is accompanied by signs every kilometre announcing the elevation and average gradient. I laugh at the drawing of a cyclist on the sign and the angle he's riding. Looks pretty steep to me. Sooner than I expect, I have only five kilometres to the summit and the gradient increases yet again. The Scotch Bloom is yellowing the meadows and I can hear cow bells from above. There are still no other cyclists, just an occasional farmer's van. I'm riding with one hand on the handlebars, the other on my camera.

With four kilometres to go, I have decided that if I was allowed to ride only one road for the rest of my life, this would be it. While my favourite climb is Col de la Croix der Fer in the French Alps, I wouldn't want to take on that beast every day.

I can see myself wheeling my bike out of the shed at Arreau and ascending this gem every morning. The beauty of Aspin is that it links two major mountain climbs - Tourmalet on the west side and Peyresourde to the east. Perhaps that explains its regular appearance on the Tour. I prefer to think the organisers know a great road when they ride it.

Three kilometres to go. The Spanish mountains are at my rear, to my left the Pic de Neouvielle rears above the clouds and the sign tells me it's 8% time. I have deliberately slowed to enjoy the view. My bike, Murray laughs disdainfully. He knows my knees are creaking.

The names of Tour riders are painted on the road surface, as with many famous climbs. But near the top, in yellow paint is one addition. ETA. The Basque Separatist Group are obviously not adverse to getting free publicity every time the peloton climb here.

I look ahead. There are definitely cows on the summit. With one kilometre to go, I increase my cadence from slow to demi-slow. As I near the pass, the cow bells sound as if to trumpet my arrival.

Merci, vache.

As I crest the top, artfully dodging cow pats and two motorcyclists, I gasp in awe at the views. Snow-capped peaks front and back, meadows and walking trails to my left and a steep pasture rearing up to my right. A cow waltzes across the road to stand beside me and admire the view.

'Nice place you have here,' I say.

He appears to nod before walking off to chew on some more lush mountain pasture. Unlike yesterday on the Col du Tourmalet, I want to dwell on this summit for as long as possible. It's astoundingly beautiful with the warm sunshine and remarkable views. It's as pleasant a place as I imagine there is on this planet to sit in the grass and linger.

A dark-haired woman in hiking clothes approaches and offers to take my photo. I stand behind Murray, his black paint job gleaming in the morning sunshine. She asks me if I'd take a photo of her. I nod readily. Before I do, she indicates for me to loan her Murray for the shot. We both laugh. She stands demurely beside Murray and smiles. Before handing Murray back, she lifts him, saying something in French, which I imagine means, 'It's light.'

Or maybe, 'It must be easy to climb with a bike that doesn't weigh much.'

Murray prefers to think she said, 'He is beautiful and so athletic!'

I'd love to stay here longer but the summit is becoming crowded with motorcyclists and cars, everyone getting out for quick snaps of the surrounding peaks before speeding off.

I reluctantly descend. For the first time ever, I overtake a van. Murray is more agile than any cumbersome tourist home. We speed off before I come to my senses and apply the brakes. I'd rather look at the views than race German tourists. We slow down and stop near a stone wall, admiring the grazing sheep in the pasture below. I take a long sip of water and let the tourist home roll slowly past.

Five kilometres from the summit, I turn a corner and come face to wheel with twenty cows being lead up the road by a shepherd wearing the obligatory Basque cap. I stop and hop off the bike, keeping Murray between me and the horns of the lead bull, just in case. The shepherd strolls casually behind the last cow with a long wooden staff in his hand. For a brief moment I consider switching jobs. To wander endlessly in these meadows...

All too soon I'm back in Arreau. It's a delightful village of tree-lined rushing streams and stone bridges. In the main street is a bar serving crepes. I can't resist. I enter and am greeted by a handsome woman with long blonde hair, wearing a white blouse and tight jeans. I order a galette with jambon and fromage. Despite the early hour, I order a celebratory beer. The crepe and the beer go down a treat. Afterwards, I step back into the sunshine and wander the streets wheeling Murray beside me.

We're on the lookout for a real estate office.

To ride this road every day. I can always dream.

Col d'Aspin is a category one climb of 12.5 kilometres from Arreau with an average gradient of 6.5% and an elevation gain of 789 metres.

Accommodation: Hotel d'Etigny, 3 Ave Paul Bonnemaison, Luchon. Friendly hosts, good comfortable rooms, wifi (best reception in the lobby), good value, if you can get a special deal. Excellent dinner but an average breakfast. Double 48 euros, breakfast extra. My score: 16/20

Restaurant: La Crepe d'Aure, 19 Grande rue, Arreau. Tasty good value crepes and galettes, friendly hosts, cosy atmosphere. My score: 15/20.

Distance cycled: 25 km

What I should have said: 'I like cows, who doesn't like cows. Please let me be a shepherd.'

Chapter Seventeen

Cirque de Gavarnie

I returned Murray to the cycle cemetery yesterday afternoon. The owner was working on an old steel road bike, painted British racing green. On the wall above the bikes hung a signed yellow jersey of Miguel Induran. The name of the shop is Casa de Miguel. I happily paid him thirty euros, as agreed, for the two extra days climbing with Murray who had been a faithful companion.

This morning, after breakfast at the friendly boulangerie on the outskirts of Luchon, Cathie and I drive through the valley and out to the motorway in an extended loop to the ski town of Luz Saint Sauveur. The shorter route is a stunning drive over the mountains I've climbed in the past three days - Peyresourde, Aspin and Tourmalet - but the road down from the summit of Tourmalet to Luz has been damaged by flood and will be impassable for the next six months at least. So we detour via the town of Lourdes, a miracle of pilgrims and tacky souvenir shops.

Luz is the starting point of the eastern climb of Col du Tourmalet and its economy is heavily dependent on cyclists in summer. In a terrible few days of mayhem and destruction a fortnight ago, the town was inundated with floodwaters surging down the mountain. As we drive into town, we see the devastation - a barn splintered and torn from its base is lodged against a tree; a car is pushed up into the ceiling of a garage, mud and debris lodged under its back wheels; farmhouses that had twenty-metre-wide frontages to the river now find the bank has crept ten metres closer; and a trail of mud and dirt seems to cover everything near the still surging river.

The streets of Luz are stained in dirt, a few shops remain closed and work crews do their best to clean up. We weren't sure whether we should come here, but the Australian owner of the hotel we'd booked assured us that what the town really needed now were tourists to help the economy and to give people something else to think about other than the events of two weeks ago. We agree, nervously.

Luz is surrounded by mountain peaks that rear up almost vertically above the town. There are numerous walking paths leading out from the town up either of the two valleys - one to the Cirque de Gavarnie, the other to Tourmalet. The town is a warren of narrow alleyways and stone houses built close to the two rivers that meet here. The roar of water remains, even weeks after the flood.

We check into our hotel early. It's in a lovely location, on a small square opposite the ancient Church of St Andrew, known locally as the Templar, which is an atmospheric pile of old stones with a small attractive church at the centre. Our host, the friendly and relaxed Sian, offers us a choice of rooms.

'We've had a few cancellations,' she explains. She looks out the window at the clear bright blue day, as if mystified why anyone would not want to come to this mountain paradise.

We choose the front room with wide windows looking out at the Templar. It's a creaky yet serene hotel with wide floorboards and solid walls, a flowering creeper climbing above the entrance and tables and chairs outside for guests to sit in the sunshine. We feel at home immediately.

As I'm not cycling today, Sian advises us to drive to Gavarnie and walk to the Cirque.

'Walk, not cycle,' I say, perhaps dumbfounded that my legs have a use other than to push pedals.

'You cyclists,' Sian laughs. 'There is more to the world than...'

'Can we take a picnic?' I interrupt. If not cycling, than food.

Sian gives us a map and also tells us about a walking path heading up to the church on the hill above Luz, 'if I can't make it to Gavarnie.' Knowing looks are exchanged between Cathie and Sian.

'What!' I bleat. 'I'll be fine without Craig.'

Is there more to life than cycling? Today I will find out.

Cathie and I load our daypack with a baguette, two local cheeses and a saucisson purchased from the local fromage shop. We have decided on a hike this morning up to the church and maybe, just maybe, Gavarnie this afternoon.

'So I'll have to carry the daypack, on my back?' I ask.

'Do you want to wheel Craig and his panniers beside you, up a hill,' Cathie answers.

I shrug on the daypack and we begin the gentle hike through the village, starting at the magnificent church which was originally built in the 12th century and fortified by the Knights Templar in the 14th century. Equal parts fort and church, it has two towers and a crenelated wall surrounding the place of worship.

The houses of the town are built of stone and painted white or left exposed, with slate roofs and brightly-painted shutters on the windows. There is barely a level piece of ground in the village, so tightly does it hug the mountainside. The front door of most houses opens out onto the road or alley. I don't fancy stumbling out early one morning, still with a hangover, only to be confronted by the admittedly infrequent and slow moving traffic.

We cross a narrow bridge over a surging stream and wind our way past a cemetery with spectacular views down the valley towards Lourdes. Some may say this vista is wasted on the inhabitants, but I prefer to imagine that every day when a loved one comes here to pay their respects, their spirits are lifted with one glance down the valley.

After thirty minutes of heavy breathing and walking at an angle, we arrive at a simple church surrounded by green grass and a few bench seats with views back down to Luz. We spread our lunch out on the seat and slowly eat the bounty of the region. Cathie smiles, knowingly.

'Okay,' I admit, 'It's almost as much fun as cycling.'

Inspired by our little foray up a hill for lunch. We drive to

Gavarnie in the afternoon and park the car outside a bar. The signs advise one hour and fifteen minutes of walking uphill will get us to the Cirque.

I don't even know what the heck a Cirque is?

Cathie leads, I dawdle behind. We have jettisoned the daypack and now carry only a bottle of water. There appears to be lots of insanely fit and well-kitted out walkers all heading in the one direction, uphill. We follow, sheepishly. I'm wearing casual sneakers and Cathie has thin-soled shoes. We are not prepared. So we do the only sensible thing. We buy a cake.

Delicious.

Now, to the Cirque! The gravel path is wide and runs alongside the delightful Gave de Pau stream. Strung out alongside the first five hundred metres of this walk are numerous restaurants and cafes selling crepes and *produit regionaux* and beer and cake and...

'Why don't we have a beer,' I suggest, 'We can look at the Cirque from here.'

Cathie wisely ignores me and we keep walking uphill, our focus on the sheer rock wall circling in front of us. A quick check of my smartphone tells me that the Cirque de Gavarnie is eight hundred metres across at the lowest point and a whopping three thousand metres wide at the top. It's a massive curtain of sheer rock circled in cloud and laced with waterfalls. The Gavarnie Falls is the highest waterfall in France at four hundred and twenty-two metres and is fed by snowmelt and a glacier on the Spanish side of the border.

Enough phone cheating.

Our walk continues over a scrambling hill and through a lovely forest. At one point, we stroll behind a couple being carried up here by donkey. Now why didn't I think of that! We stop and look back down the stream towards the cafes and the lovely stone bridge arching over the rushing snowmelt. It's postcard perfect. I check my watch. Only fifteen minutes to the top, if the signs can be believed.

It's entirely appropriate that Cathie leads me into the final climb.

On the canal section of our bike journey, she scaled every hill no matter what the distance or gradient, always trailing stoically behind. I'd wait at the top and offer encouraging words.

Now she does the same. She knows just what to say.

'Look, there's a pub up ahead.'

I can't believe it, but the wise and thoughtful French have constructed a plain double-storey hotel not far from the base of the Cirque. Tables and chairs are arranged under umbrellas with expansive views of the imposing wall of mountain looming over us. We celebrate with a few glasses of Kronenbourg.

What a view.

What a walk.

What a beer.

We take photo after photo. Me with Cirque. Me with beer and Cirque. Cathie with Cirque. A selfie of Cathie and half-my-head, with Cirque.

According to the literature on display, one of the most prominent features of the Cirque is the La Breche de Roland, a natural gap cleaved into the top of the mountainside. Legend has it that Count Roland cut this gap with his sword Durendal in a failed attempt to destroy the weapon after being defeated at the Battle of Roncevaux Pass. Durendal was delivered by an angel to Charlemagne who gave it to his cousin Roland. The sword proved indestructible and Roland was forced to live with it.

'Perhaps I should rename Craig, Durendal,' I say.

'You think of Craig more than you think of me, don't you,' Cathie smiles.

'How about another beer, my darling,' I answer.

We sit under the expansive awning of the Cirque de Gavarnie, talking of indestructible swords and bicycles and wondering if we can hire a donkey for the return journey back to our car.

Accommodation: Hotel Les Templiers, 6 Place de le Comporte

(Place de l'Eglise), Luz Saint Sauveur. Friendly relaxed hosts, excellent breakfast, comfortable rooms, wifi, perfect location. Double 55-65 Euros, breakfast extra. My score: 17/20.

Restaurant: Restaurant Chez Christine, 3 rue d'Ossun Prolongee, Luz Saint Sauveur. A family run bolt-hole of a restaurant and pizzeria that is great value with delicious simple meals in a pleasant atmosphere. The pizzas are crusty thin base marvels with quirky but appetising toppings (apple and goats cheese anyone?). The restaurant also offers more traditional meals like magret de canard and poulet. My score: 17/20.

Distance walked: Too far!

What I should have said: 'How much for that donkey, good man?'

Chapter Eighteen

Col d'Aubisque

After enjoying the delicious breakfast at Hotel Les Templiers this morning, I can rank it as perhaps the best petit dejeuner I've had in France. Organic muesli and fruit, yoghurt, fresh croissants, wholemeal bread and the obligatory baguette, washed down with good coffee. Enough sustenance to cycle up a mountain, surely?

For my final mountain climb of this trip, I have chosen Col d'Aubisque, one of the legendary climbs of the Tour de France. So legendary in fact that it was included in the Grande Boucle every year from its debut in 1910 until 1977. Astonishing!

I have a new climbing partner today. A Dutch bike painted black and silver, from the Focus company. I hope he's not related to the horrible Prog-Rock band of the 1970's, also called Focus. I quickly offer my friend a new name, Tjalling, in honour of the translator of my books in The Netherlands. When I'm not riding a bike, I'm an author of books for children and young adults and Tjalling has done a sterling job on four of my novels.

In cold but clear conditions, Tjalling and I set out from Argeles-Gavost, a lovely village in the Pyrenees. The first few kilometres are hardly welcoming, offering a brutal 8.5% gradient. I'm being tailed by two riders who are gratefully getting assistance at the start. When we reach level ground in the Val d'Azun, they swing past me and suggest our own little peloton. I say, 'Non, merci.' The truth is I always feel as if I'm pushing too hard when riding with other cyclists. I'm not here for a time trial. I prefer to enjoy the views and the exercise. And the beer at the finish. They speed off and I'm left alone with Tjalling who has an aluminium frame and carbon forks, so he's a touch heavier than I've had in the past few days. But after last night's magret de canard, so am I.

The valley road takes me through lovely peaceful villages, each with a church and a rushing stream of snowmelt. I'm a little confused. I expected more serious climbing. The gradient slips between 2% and 6%, all relatively easy. I cycle beside lush meadows dotted with trees and ringed by stone walls. It's a serene valley surrounded by gentle green hills, not the fearsome mountain I'd expected. Truth is, I haven't read enough about the climb beforehand to know what to expect. Cycling through this peaceful valley only increases my foreboding of what lies ahead. For a hors category mountain, it's doing a good job of pretending to be an infant category five.

I cycle through the narrow streets of Aucun and see the snow-capped mountains rearing before me along the Route d'Azun. Oh dear. I stop to fill my water bottle. I may need all the refreshment I can get.

I cycle into the village of Arrens which features a simple white-painted church with a wooden portico and is surrounded by stone walls topped with flower boxes. On the outskirts of town, a sign tells me that the Col du Soulor begins here with an impressive 8% rise. I'm aware I have to climb Soulor before d'Aubisque. I guess that means I can claim I've climbed two mountains in the one morning? If I make it. I've ridden twelve kilometres and still have eighteen more to the summit. Soulor offers no respite, with slow looping bends and a gradient that doesn't drop below 7%.

To my left are mountains shrouded in cloud. A stone barn appears every few hundred metres. For sheltering animals in winter, I imagine. I round a bend and see the most attractive rubbish bin I'm ever like to encounter. Built of stone, it's backed by a pine forest and has an excellent view down into the valley. All for the rubbish.

After what seems like an eternity of climbing, I reach the summit of Soulor. It's taken more energy than I'd expected to make it up here. I'm greeted by one of the cyclists who offered a peloton earlier. He congratulates me and advises me to wear a jacket and eat something before continuing. Do I look that bad?

He explains that the road now descends for three kilometres before climbing again to d'Aubisque. In other words, I'm now going to freeze on the downhill, wasting valuable metres while my muscles seize up. I walk into the cafe and buy a sugary soft drink. I can't stomach food at the moment. I just need quick energy.

I shouldn't have worried. As soon as I drop down over the Soulor summit, I see the road ahead. The tarmac descends steeply, hugging the outside of a mountain before turning left. After one kilometre, I stop. I am gobsmacked by the view. Ahead of me, the thin bitumen route I'll be riding is seemingly chiselled into the side of a mountain. It's like an asphalt balcony. What's even more exciting is the gradient doesn't appear to be too steep. I'll be riding along a narrow platform, halfway up a mountain with sweeping views to the valley below and mountains opposite. I take a photo, but I know it won't do justice to the view.

It's an unforgettable ride. Craggy peaks loom directly above the road, which along the balcony offers such an easy gradient, I can relax and enjoy the vista. To my right, two hawks chase each other across the valley until they are only a hundred metres from me. Then suddenly, one hawk drops, falling swiftly for fifty metres, followed by his acrobatic partner. Wow! I almost ride off the road, so entranced am I by the aerial display. The 'safety rails' are sixty-centimetre stone blocks. They're not stopping a wayward cyclist from a sheer drop to the valley below.

The first tunnel is short and perfectly frames a mountain ahead. The second tunnel is pitch black, damp and I cannot see the road I'm riding on. I hope there are no rocks ahead.

I'm riding along the Cirque de Litor, perhaps one of the most filmed and photographed sections of the Tour de France. It's awe-inspiringly beautiful. I cycle very slowly, looking up to the jagged rocks rearing above me, then down to the valley below where a stream snakes through the green meadows. After a few minutes, I realise I'm riding uphill and smiling. I'm so entranced by the scenery, I'd forgotten the gradient. I'm also very aware and very happy that I must return this way on the descent. I get to ride this magical road twice!

I enter a cool forest section for one kilometre, catch my breath and drink the last of my water. My lips are dry, not from exertion, but from excitement.

The last three kilometres are steep, as if d'Aubisque is not letting me have all this pleasure so easily. I pass a herd of cows, one is knee deep in mud beside the road. She doesn't appear concerned, munching on the grass. Finally and somewhat reluctantly, I reach the summit at 1710 metres.

The view is spectacular, although many of the mountains are cloaked in clouds. The temperature is noticeably cooler up here. Across the road from the hotel is a sculpture of three giant bicycles, each painted a colour of the Tour winning jerseys - yellow for the overall winner; green for the sprinter; white with dots for King of the Mountain. They have a lovely backdrop of snow-capped mountains. I can't resist standing Tjalling and myself in front of them for one quick snap.

I don't stay long at the summit, time enough for a coffee served by a friendly chap at the hotel. We get talking about travel, as you do. He's been to Australia and liked it so much he married one of the locals. They spend the season in this beautiful landscape of mountains and alpine meadows, making excellent coffee in a location as far removed from my flat and dry homeland as it's possible to be.

Sitting in the sun, sipping coffee, I have time to relive my climb up the Cirque de Litor. I'm eager to do it again and keep telling myself that I must descend slowly so as to savour every moment.

Tjalling has other ideas. We set off at a spine-chilling pace, so fast that it's the first time I experience a car pulling off the road to let me through because he can't go as fast on the winding narrow road. After I pass him, I realise I now have to keep up the pace. Stupid!

Three hundred metres on, I pull over and pretend to check my rear brakes until he passes. Now back to a casual dawdle. The Cirque is just as beautiful second time around. The mountains rearing above me are stark and jagged against the intensely blue sky. I keep stopping to take photos and cursing myself for not bringing my video camera that straps to the handlebars. If there's one road I'd like to film...

The three kilometre climb back up to Col du Soulor is slow and creaky. My muscles are cold from the descent and it's an effort to push myself further. At Soulor, I stop for a fromage and jambon baguette from a cheese shop. I sit at an outdoor table, looking back at the Cirque de Litor.

It's an appropriate place to finish my cycle tour of south-western France, here among the peaks and meadows, eating a delicious baguette. If only I could tempt myself with a glass of wine. Bordeaux, of course. But the descent of Soulor prevents me from indulging.

It's an easy downhill to Arrens, stopping only once to take a photo of the world's most attractive rubbish bin. As I cycle along the Route d'Aruz, I'm impressed with the number of cyclists heading towards d'Aubisque. The lure of the Cirque is world renown.

Col d'Aubisque is one of the best routes I've ever ridden. It ranks up there with Col d'Aspin and Col de la Croix de Fer. I now understand why it's used by the Tour so frequently.

In Argeles-Gavost, I stop at a bar in the town square for a beer. Cathie joins me and we sit in the sun, toasting the last few weeks, retracing our cycle tracks along the canals and through the mountains.

'I think I'll call this book, *bordeaux and bicycles*,' I suggest.

Cathie holds up her glass of red and clinks my beer, 'Shouldn't it be *beer and bicycles*,' she adds.

'Vineyard, river, vineyard, canal, vineyard, mountain,' I say, by way of explanation.

Cathie considers it for a moment and then nods agreement.

'What about next year?' she asks.

'I like your suggestion of the Danube, by bicycle,' I say.

'Bratwurst and bicycles,' she laughs.

I order another beer for myself and a bordeaux for my beautiful wife, who on this trip has discovered a love of cycling equal to my own. Bless her.

Col d'Aubisque is a hors category climb in the Pyrenees of thirty kilometres with an elevation of 1710 metres and an average gradient 4.1% and an elevation gain of 1247 metres.

Don't be fooled by the low average gradient. Ten kilometres are along the valley floor. If you removed these from the equation, the average gradient would be between 6% and 7%.

Accommodation: Hotel Les Templiers, 6 Place de le Comporte (Place de l'Eglise), Luz Saint Sauveur. Friendly relaxed hosts, excellent breakfast, comfortable rooms, wifi, perfect location. Double 55-65 Euros, breakfast extra. My score: 17/20.

Restaurant: Restaurant Chez Christine, 3 rue d'Ossun Prolongee, Luz Saint Sauveur. A family run bolt-hole of a restaurant and pizzeria that is great value with delicious simple meals in a pleasant atmosphere. The pizzas are crusty thin base marvels with quirky but appetising toppings (apple and goats cheese anyone?). The restaurant also offers more traditional meals like magret de canard and poulet. My score: 17/20.

Distance cycled: 61 km

What I should have said: 'A bottle of bordeaux, s'il vous plait? For the flight home.'

Printed in Great Britain
by Amazon

17926502R00071